William P. Smith gets right to the cry of my heart in his latest book, *Assurance: Resting in God's Salvation*, when he asks, "Are you used to thinking of God as someone who cares about doubters?" What a perfect question to help us all to meditate on and proclaim the scriptural truth that God delights in helping doubters to grow in assurance of his love.

—**Tara Barthel**, Professional Christian Mediator; Author, the *Living the Gospel in Relationships* DVD Series

Bill Smith is enthralled by the gospel. I have heard him teach and preach, read his articles and books, and counseled with him. His "laser-like," soul-piercing questions and his gentle naming of the struggle to understand and believe God's benevolent grace are accurate, because he has first identified the same struggles to believe in his own heart. This 31-day devotional has isolated and addressed the most difficult questions that I often revisit in my own mind. It helps me by softening my heart so that, awed again by God, I believe.

—**Penny Nelson Freeman**, Counselor, ServingLeaders Ministries; Counselor and Trainer, Parakaleo

Bill Smith has done a great service for those who feel the absence of God in the presence of our suffering, our sorrow, and even our battle with sin. Each daily reading offers fresh perspective, unshackling insights, and biblical wisdom that focuses the mind and fortifies the soul. If you feel a pressing need to live with an assurance of the astounding scope of God's love, take a month and allow *Assurance* to enrich your faith in God. Then do it again!

—**Dave Harvey**, Teaching Pastor, Summit Church, Naples, Florida; Author, *When Sinners Say "I Do": Discovering the Power of the Gospel for Marriage*

As I began reading Bill Smith's devotional, *A̶s̶s̶u̶r̶a̶n̶c̶e̶: ̶R̶e̶s̶t̶i̶n̶g̶ ̶i̶n̶ God's Salvation*, people who I ca̶n̶

D0869523

mind. Whether they are counselees, members of my church, or extended family members, so many Christians who I know struggle with feeling assurance of their salvation. Now that I have finished *Assurance*, I can't wait to share copies of it with these dear folks. Bill does not ignore our doubts or diminish our feelings. Instead, he consistently, gently, and wisely shepherds us back to *the* Shepherd and the Scriptures.

> —**Bob Kellemen**, Vice President of Strategic Development and Academic Dean, Faith Bible Seminary, Lafayette, Indiana; Author, *Grief: Walking with Jesus*

This is one of the most refreshing devotionals I have read in quite some time. Bill is a skilled pastor, counselor, and apologist for the Christian faith. Throughout this 31-day devotional, he condenses rich biblical doctrine into bite-size truths and applies them to common doubts that most Christians wrestle with. This was a deep encouragement to my soul, and I trust it will be to yours as well. Highly recommended!

> —**John Perritt**, Director of Resources, Reformed Youth Ministries; Author, *Insecure: Fighting Our Lesser Fears with a Greater One*

I'm convinced that virtually every true Christian doubts his or her salvation on occasion. After all, if we have an entire book of the Bible—namely, 1 John—written to address the subject, you can be sure it's a common problem in the Christian life. If you're holding this book because you struggle with whether you are right with God, I believe you will find solid, biblical help in these pages.

> —**Donald S. Whitney**, Professor of Biblical Spirituality and Associate Dean of the School of Theology, The Southern Baptist Theological Seminary, Louisville, Kentucky; Author, *How Can I Be Sure I'm a Christian?*

ASSURANCE

31-DAY DEVOTIONALS FOR LIFE

A Series

DEEPAK REJU
Series Editor

Addictive Habits: Changing for Good, by David R. Dunham
After an Affair: Pursuing Restoration, by Michael Scott Gembola
Anger: Calming Your Heart, by Robert D. Jones
Anxiety: Knowing God's Peace, by Paul Tautges
Assurance: Resting in God's Salvation, by William P. Smith
Chronic Illness: Walking by Faith, by Esther Smith
Contentment: Seeing God's Goodness, by Megan Hill
Doubt: Trusting God's Promises, by Elyse Fitzpatrick
Engagement: Preparing for Marriage, by Mike McKinley
Fearing Others: Putting God First, by Zach Schlegel
Grief: Walking with Jesus, by Bob Kellemen
Marriage Conflict: Talking as Teammates, by Steve Hoppe
Money: Seeking God's Wisdom, by Jim Newheiser
Pornography: Fighting for Purity, by Deepak Reju

ASSURANCE

RESTING
IN GOD'S
SALVATION

WILLIAM P. SMITH

P&R
PUBLISHING
P.O. BOX 817 • PHILLIPSBURG • NEW JERSEY 08865-0817

Library of Congress Cataloging-in-Publication Data

Names: Smith, William P., 1965- author.
Title: Assurance : resting in God's salvation / William P. Smith.
Description: Phillipsburg : P&R Publishing, 2019. | Series: 31-day devotionals for life
Identifiers: LCCN 2018044754| ISBN 9781629954400 (pbk.) | ISBN 9781629954417 (epub) | ISBN 9781629954424 (mobi)
Subjects: LCSH: Assurance (Theology) | Devotional literature.
Classification: LCC BT785 .S58 2019 | DDC 242/.2--dc23
LC record available at https://lccn.loc.gov/2018044754

For the bruised reeds and smoldering wicks
that at times we all are.

Contents

Tips for Reading This Devotional

EARLY IN OUR marriage, my wife and I lived on the top floor of a town house, in a small one-bedroom apartment. Whenever it rained, leaks in the roof would drip through the ceiling and onto our floors. I remember placing buckets in different parts of the apartment and watching the water slowly drip, one drop at a time. I put large buckets out and thought, *It'll take a while to fill them.* The water built up over time, and often I was surprised at how quickly those buckets filled up, overflowing if I didn't pay close enough attention.

This devotional is just like rain filling up a bucket. It's slow, and it builds over time. Just a few verses every day. Drip. Drip. Drip. Just a few drops of Scripture daily to satiate your parched soul.

We start with Scripture. God's Word is powerful. In fact, it's the most powerful force in the entire universe.[1] It turns the hearts of kings, brings comfort to the lowly, and gives spiritual sight to the blind. It transforms lives and turns them upside down. We know that the Bible is God's very own words, so we read and study it to know God himself.

Our study of Scripture is practical. Theology should change how we live. It's crucial to connect the Word with your struggles. Often, as you read this devotional, you'll see the word *you* because Bill speaks directly to you, the reader. The readings contain a mixture of reflection questions and practical suggestions. You'll get much more from this experience if you answer the questions and do the practical exercises. Don't skip them. Do them for the sake of your own soul.

1. Jonathan Leeman, *Reverberation: How God's Word Brings Light, Freedom, and Action to His People* (Chicago: Moody, 2011), 19.

Our study of Scripture is worshipful. Fundamentally, any struggle with assurance is a worship problem. We've lost our orientation toward the One who should rule our lives, and we need to turn back to him. The Word points us to Christ, who rescues us from our plight and reorients our life. The goal of your time in God's Word should always be renewed worship. Even though you've struggled with doubt and uncertainty about your salvation, the Lord himself tenderly takes you by the hand and leads you along the narrow path back to him. As you grow in your affections for Christ, the King, hope and certainty grow. A greater love for Christ transforms your soul. Adore Christ. Love him. Cherish him. Praise him. Honor him. Give your whole life to him. Don't hold anything back.

If you find this devotional helpful (and I trust that you will!), reread it in different seasons of your life. Work through it this coming month, and then come back to it a year from now, to continue growing more deeply assured that God really has rescued and saved you.

This devotional is *not* meant to be a comprehensive guide to struggles with assurance. Good volumes are already written for that purpose. Buy them and make good use of them. You'll see several resources listed at the end of the book.

That's enough for now. Let's begin.

Deepak Reju

Introduction

WHY WOULD YOU doubt God's promises to you? Why would you struggle to believe that he loves you, is actively at work in you, is planning good things for you, and is delighting in you? In short, why is it so difficult to be certain that he has saved you?

The answer is easy: sometimes it just doesn't look like it, because the evidence of your life seems to argue for a different conclusion.

For instance, you still go through hard times. Bad things happen to you, and people hurt you. You still suffer. And so it feels logical to wonder, "If God is as powerful as he says he is, then he could have stopped these things from happening to me if he really loved me . . . so maybe that means he doesn't?"

Or you look at the things you don't have—a spouse, children, a satisfying career, fun vacations, the latest electronics, a nicely decorated home, a healthy bank account, or a healthy body—and you think, "Other people seem to be far better off than I am. If God blesses his people, and if I'm not blessed . . . maybe that means I'm not one of his people?"

Or, worse, you look at what comes out of your life. You do things that you know are wrong—things that you feel guilty about—but things that you can't seem to stop doing. Doubt creeps in and asks, "If the sparkle and tug of sin feel so much more attractive than the glory of God does, how can you possibly be a child of his?"

And you start nodding your head in agreement. It only makes sense to think, "If what comes out of me bears little resemblance to the work of the Holy Spirit, then doesn't it follow that I'm not being led by the Spirit? And if I'm not being led by him, doesn't that mean I am more active and involved in my life than he is? So maybe that means he's not in me."

Being certain—assured—that God has saved you from sin

and destruction, and has made you part of his glorious New Creation, is never a matter of theological information only. It's an existential problem that's created when the data of your life doesn't line up with what you believe the new life in Christ should be. At those times, uncertainty makes sense.

Now, it's relatively easy to challenge the *logic* of doubt (for example: how many times do you think you can be reborn?), but the *feeling* of doubt is what's so compelling and stubborn. Unfortunately, many people attempt to deal with their uncertainty by looking at the same things that caused them to feel uncertain in the first place. They look to see whether their circumstances improve or whether their failure rate drops.

The antidote to doubt, however, never comes as a result of increasing your gaze outward to your circumstances or focusing inward on yourself. It comes when you look more intently upward to a God who moves toward you in order to live with you. Your doubts tempt you to move away from him or from anything that reminds you of him. But those are precisely the times when you need to look even more intently into Scripture to see a God who longs to help his people deal with their fear and uncertainty.

Sometimes, in the Bible, the Lord challenges people—and you, as you read it—directly, in the "Why do you have so little faith?" passages. More often, however, he gives you pictures, metaphors, descriptions, and explanations of what he's been doing on your behalf to help you understand that he's not demoralized by you or ready to quit and give up on you. Instead, he really believes he will be successful in rescuing you from yourself, and he wants you to have the same confidence that he has. Passages like these pull back the curtain on his heart so that you can see how much he loves you and longs for you, even when you're not sure that he does.

Discovering a God who talks to you about your doubt helps you to realize that he always knew you would experience that doubt. Far from being offended by your doubt, he anticipated it, offering you answers before you even existed to have questions.

If you're not sure that God has saved you and is working in your life, it's because you believe that the momentary, fleeting things of this life have more influence in you and on you than does the God who made you, redeems you, and sustains you. That means that, in order to address doubt, you need to see the world in a whole new light. You need to embed each thing that provokes your uncertainty within the larger framework of a God who, at great personal cost to himself, set his love on you through Christ so that you would only ever be with him.

In order to address your lack of assurance, you need to see

- God's heart for you, as expressed through his character and his actions toward people who doubt,
- the resources that he gives you to tackle the things that are urging you to doubt him and his goodness, and
- how impotent any doubt-producing thing is in light of God's unstoppable power.

That's my aim in this book. I am not addressing theological issues regarding doubt in general (for example, *How can there be only one way to know God?*). Rather, I am focusing on doubts about God's goodness as it specifically relates to you, as a particular individual (for example, *I believe that God loves humanity, but I'm not so sure that he loves me—so how can I be sure that his promises apply to me?*).

Personal questions about the status of your relationship with God require knowing things about him, and yet assurance is ultimately not a matter of what you know. The problem is that you don't believe what you know. Growing in assurance, then, is not a matter of simply getting more information. It's a matter of trust. It's a matter of believing the character of the one who is trying to communicate information to you.

When telemarketers call and promise me the cruise of a lifetime for next to nothing, I hang up. I don't know them. I don't trust them, and frankly, I want nothing to do with them—and no amount of information will change that.

When my wife calls, however, and invites me to take a walk with her after work, I rearrange my evening's plans and can't get home quickly enough. What's the difference? I know her and trust her, and because of that, I want more of her.

My hope is that, as you see God engage you in your uncertainty, you'll know him better, grow to trust him more, and develop a greater hunger for him.

ACKNOWLEDGING
YOUR UNCERTAINTIES

DAY 1

"How Can God Forgive Me after What I've Done?"

"I will put enmity between you and the woman, and between your offspring and her offspring; he shall bruise your head, and you shall bruise his heel." (Gen. 3:15)

EVERYONE'S CONSCIENCE HAS a different setting. Some of us are more sensitive and don't have to do much before we are deeply upset with ourselves—such as speaking harshly, slapping our child in anger, shoplifting something small, or drinking too much the night before. Others of us are more hardened and need more in order to convict us that we're out of line—such as cheating on our spouse, embezzling from the family business, ruining someone's reputation, or chiseling a relative out of their inheritance.

The particulars are unique to each person, but what is universal is that there is at least one thing you have done that creeps into your mind at the oddest times, when your guard is down. Something you just can't let go of—that you think about far more often than you'd like. Something that you find unforgivable.

No one needs to point it out to you, because your conscience points it out. And because it lingers there in your conscience, you start to wonder, "If I can't forgive myself, how can God forgive me?"

That's when it's helpful to consider the first human sin, back in the garden of Eden. The results of that sin were catastrophic: It plunged all of humanity into sin, so that we're each born separated from the God in whose image we are made (see Eph. 2:1–3). It bound every one of our race to an inescapable death (see Rom. 5:12–14). It subjected the entire universe to the curse of frustration and decay, so that nothing works or lasts the way that

17

it should (see Rom. 8:20–21). Nothing you have done or ever will do can begin to compare with the tragedy that Adam and Eve wrote for the rest of their descendants.

But God didn't sit back and watch the story unfold to its logical conclusion. He inserted himself into it—and, by doing so, rewrote the ending. He interposed hatred between our first foreparents and their enemy, the Serpent—signaling that he would turn their hearts back to him—and he promised to send the Snake-Crusher so that sin and evil would not have the last word (see Gen. 3:15).

He didn't abandon Adam and Eve to their fate—which gives you confidence that he won't abandon you to yours. He doesn't merely forgive; he throws himself into the fray, using all his power and energy to rewrite the tragic story that his people had crafted for themselves. And he does this not just for humanity as a whole but for you, as an individual, as well.

The question has never been "How good are you at being good?" It has always been "How good is God at being good when you are not?" Let yourself be captured, then, not only by the depth of his goodness but also by its breadth. Watch as his goodness outstrips the destruction that sin has brought cosmically, and your confidence will grow in how he responds to you personally.

Reflect: Think about the thing that most haunts your conscience. How does its result compare in size or scope to that of the first human sin?

Reflect: What do you think is more powerful: your ability to ruin your life, or God's ability to rescue and restore it? (Hint: which do you spend more time thinking about?)

Act: Spend a few minutes talking to God about what he does in relation to what you have done.

DAY 2

"I Can't Stop Thinking about What I've Done"

For I know my transgressions,
and my sin is ever before me. (Ps. 51:3)

THE ENEMIES OF your soul are not only relentless but also dishonest. They play both sides of sin against you.

First, they flood your mind and inflame your heart with non-stop temptation, promising that if you'll just give in, then your life will be better than you could imagine. Then, when you do give in and enjoy the fleeting pleasure of sin (see Heb. 11:25), they flood you with a different barrage.

This time, the thoughts that you can't get away from run along such lines as "How could you? Look at what you've done. You know better. You call yourself a Christian? God couldn't possibly love you." Your heart is heavy. There's no joy in the world, and everything looks bleak.

That's what God's enemies do. They provoke you in order to goad you toward a destructive cliff. Then, when you take the bait and plunge over the edge, they stand there accusing you of your failure just as loudly as they once urged you toward it.

King David has been there. The man after God's own heart (see 1 Sam. 13:14) became infatuated with another man's wife. He couldn't get her out of his mind, invited her over, slept with her, made a baby with her, and then murdered her husband so he could marry her in order to cover it all up.

For a time, it looked like he'd gotten away with it. But when God confronted him about it through the prophet Nathan, David couldn't get out of his mind what he'd done. "My sin is ever before me"—can you hear how keenly aware he is of it? There's no escape from it. He sees it everywhere he goes, and he hates it. What once was not a big deal now haunts him.

But while the problem consumes his mind and his heart, he doesn't stay locked up inside himself. That would be foolish. Since his mind and heart got him into trouble, they won't be much help in getting him out. And so he doesn't keep trying to deal with the mess or to figure out how to make things right on his own. Instead, he runs to God.

He doesn't go to God in order to hear the same thoughts that come from within him—the thoughts that accuse and condemn him. Instead he goes to God for mercy (see Ps. 51:1), for compassion (see v. 1), for cleansing (see v. 2), for a clean heart (see vv. 7, 10), for God's renewed presence in his life (see vv. 11–12) and for freedom from guilt (see v. 14) so that he can praise God once again (see v. 15).

He goes to God not on the strength of what *he* could do to make things right with God (see v. 16) but on the strength of what *God* does to make things right between David and himself (see vv. 7–12) according to God's unfailing love (see v. 1).

The presence of sin in David's life doesn't drive him to doubt God's love; it drives him to seek the God who loves him.

Reflect: What does the ugliness of David's sin tell you about the greatness of God's grace?

Reflect: What does the goodness that David experiences tell you about God's longing to restore things between himself and his people?

Act: You can grow in confidence only by experiencing this grace—so, like David, let the sin that is ever before you drive you to God rather than away from him. Use David's prayer in Psalm 51 to frame your own.

DAY 3

"But I Keep Sinning!"

*"For I the Lord do not change; therefore you, O children of Jacob,
are not consumed. From the days of your fathers you have turned
aside from my statutes and have not kept them. Return to me, and
I will return to you, says the Lord of hosts." (Mal. 3:6–7)*

HAVE YOU EVER thought something like "I came to Christ
because I saw my sin for what it was and I hated it. I was so happy
to be forgiven and set free—but now I find myself doing things
that I hate and know I'll regret. How can I be a Christian if I keep
falling into the same patterns?"

This is a common trap. You fall into it when you try to prove
your justification (the fact that you've been set right with God
through Christ's sacrifice) by examining your sanctification
(whether you are now living more righteously).

Many Christians understand that justification produces sanctification, but it's easy to forget that, while justification happens
in an instant, sanctification is a lifelong process—one that is often
nonlinear as you run into roadblocks and experience setbacks. If
you expect to see some evidence of the end result (sinless perfec-
tion) while skipping over the process, you will be disappointed—
and, worse, you will question how effective your sanctification is.
Those questions will then lead you to wonder whether you were
ever justified.

Here's why you can't prove that you've been justified by mea-
suring your sanctification: on this earth, you will never get to a
place of sinlessness (see 1 John 1:8). The sin nature still resides
inside you, and it strives against the Spirit of God (see Gal. 5:17).
And so even the godliest Christians find themselves doing things
that they no longer want to do (see Rom. 7:15–20; Gal. 2:11–13).

If sinlessness is a precondition for knowing that we're saved, then none of us qualify. Our inclination to see things this way is merely another trick of the Evil One to keep us focused on the object of salvation (us) and not on its author (God).

Malachi 3:6–7 offers a different focus. God acknowledges that his people have always had a problem being faithful to him. His response is not to be disgusted with us, to throw his hands up and walk away, to threaten us, to tell us to work harder, or to offer us bribes so we will be good. Instead he offers us an invitation. He invites us to turn back to him, despite having sinned just like our ancestors. He doesn't base that invitation on the strength of how hard we are trying or how successful we are. He bases it on his unchanging nature. He is the God who made us to know him— to love him and be loved by him. He has never wavered from his desire for us to do so, despite the many reasons we have given and continue to give him.

He still wants you. What you have done has not changed what he already did for you. Nor has it changed his heart for you. He doesn't want you to wonder if he has turned from you. Rather, he longs for you to turn to him.

Reflect: Have you fallen into the trap of evaluating God's effectiveness at justifying you by how well you are living a holy life? What makes that trap appealing to you?

Reflect: God's unchangeableness means that he keeps wooing you back when you stray, just as he did before you first turned to him. When was the last time you told him how amazed you are at his commitment to you?

Act: Go to a trusted friend and talk about the unchanging invitation God offers to turn back to him.

DAY 4

The Unforgivable Sin

"Whoever is not with me is against me, and whoever does not gather with me scatters. Therefore I tell you, every sin and blasphemy will be forgiven people, but the blasphemy against the Spirit will not be forgiven." (Matt. 12:30–31)

THE DIFFICULTY WITH doubt is that it's irrationally stubborn and doesn't submit well to logic. Take, for instance, Jesus's statement that you can be forgiven for anything except speaking against the Holy Spirit. You may have heard that this unpardonable sin means giving credit to evil for something that the Holy Spirit is doing and steadfastly refusing to see it otherwise—like claiming that Jesus got his power to cast out demons from the prince of demons and not from God's Spirit (see Matt. 12:24). But if you have a sensitive conscience or you once explicitly rejected Christ, then that explanation may not relieve your anxiety.

If that's the case, then let's think together. If you really have done what God considers unforgivable, who cares? That's a serious question—I'm not making light of your concern. Obviously you care. But who else?

Satan? No; he'd be thrilled. Any of his underlings? No again; you would have just made their job easier. How about your unbelieving relatives, neighbors, coworkers, or acquaintances? Again, still no. They may not celebrate what you've done, but frankly, they won't care about an issue between you and God as long as it doesn't affect them.

Does God care, though? Absolutely. That's why he talked about the unforgivable sin on earth and preserved this passage in Scripture. How about the angels in heaven? Again, yes; they go wild in heaven when a sinner repents (see Luke 15:10). Do

23

your believing friends care? Of course they do. How about your pastor, elder, small-group leader, counselor, and anyone else who watches over your soul? All of them do.

In other words, when you think about those who may be interested in whether you are beyond forgiveness, you discover a distinction: no power or representative of the kingdom of darkness cares, while all those who are in the kingdom of light do.

So if you care that you may have eternally offended God without the hope of being pardoned and you can't stand the thought, what does that tell you about which kingdom you are part of? It's pretty clear that it's not the kingdom of darkness—but then that leaves you only one other possibility: the kingdom of light. And if you are, in fact, representing the kingdom of light in the way that you're feeling and responding, how did you become part of it?

Only by being forgiven.

Apparently, then, whatever you've done, God considered it forgivable.

Reflect: Have you considered before that those in the kingdom of light care more for you than those in the kingdom of darkness do? Does that way of thinking make sense to you?

Reflect: When your concerns about sin line up with God's concerns, what does that tell you about what he's done in you?

Act: Practice letting thankfulness replace your fear. Tell God how thankful you are that he's given you a heart that cares about what he thinks. Thank him that you can't stand the thought of missing out on being with him. Thank him that you now care about being forgiven, and then allow your thankfulness to push out your worries and concerns.

DAY 5

"If God Really Loved Me, He Wouldn't Let Bad Things Happen to Me"

For I consider that the sufferings of this present time are not worth comparing with the glory that is to be revealed to us. (Rom. 8:18)

THE WORLD IS full of ugliness, and although we may not have met, I know that you've experienced your fair share of it—or, perhaps, more than what's fair. And I know that's been true even since you've come to Christ and started calling God *Father*.

And that's troubling. How can you be certain that God loves you if he lets bad things happen to you? If he loves you, you are supposed to be his child, right? After all, if you had the power, wouldn't you protect your child from as much evil as possible? God certainly doesn't seem to protect you from all the evil he could. And that lets doubt creep in around the edges, leaving you wondering just how much he really does love you.

How do you learn not to gauge God's pleasure with you by the ease or dis-ease of your life? As with everything else in the Christian life, it goes back to looking at Jesus.

God made sure everyone knew that he was not merely pleased with Jesus but well-pleased (see Matt. 3:17). The Father delighted in him as he delighted in nothing and no one else. Yet Jesus endured a miserably difficult life that ended in a death he asked not to go through—knowing all along that the Father not only allowed it but orchestrated it (see John 19:11).

Why then did Jesus go through all that? Because he saw the joy on the other end (see Heb. 12:2) and thought that what was offered was so worthwhile that it made the cross bearable. He was captured by the joy of rescuing and redeeming his runaway creation so that he and it—which includes you and the rest of God's children—would be reunited with each other and with the Father.

His suffering was necessary in order to accomplish God's good purposes. Remember that he essentially asked the Father, "Is there any other way except the cross?" (see Mark 14:36). The silence of God's answer spoke loudly: "No. This is the only possibility."

If there was no other possibility for Christ except to suffer, and if you are now connected to him—"in Christ," as Paul puts it; or, as Jesus says even more personally, "in me"—then, by extension, there is no other possibility for you either. God's love for you and the suffering you face in this world are not mutually exclusive. In fact, if God loves you, you are promised suffering (see Acts 14:22).

How do you navigate that hard reality with hope? It calls for patient endurance (see Rev. 13:10)—the kind that believes that God's plan is so glorious that in the end it will wipe away the memory of any and all pain (see Rom. 8:18), despite that pain's having been necessary to achieve the glory you will enjoy (see Rom. 8:17, 28–30).

Reflect: Spend some time meditating on the fact that God both loved his one and only Son and also prepared a life of suffering for him. Ask God to give you insight into this mystery.

Act: Pick an area of life that is hard for you right now, and instead of asking, "Why me?" regarding that area, practice praying, "Your will be done. Father, give me faith to believe that what you've planned and allowed is better than any other life I would have chosen for myself."

DAY 6

"Why Does God Let Bad People Get Away with Hurting Me?"

But as for me, my feet had almost stumbled, my steps had nearly slipped. For I was envious of the arrogant when I saw the prosperity of the wicked. (Ps. 73:2–3)

IT'S HARD TO believe that God loves you when he lets bad things happen to you. It's even harder when he lets good things happen to bad people who hurt you.

The news is full of people who do horrible things to others: conning them, defrauding them, using their position to take what they want—and then getting away with it, often for years, becoming even more rich and powerful.

But you don't need impersonal news stories to provoke your doubt; you have stories of your own. Times when people took advantage of you—a friend, a relative, a coworker, a contractor—and it left them better off than they were before. God is supposed to be all-powerful and completely good—but you got hurt, and those who were responsible ended up better off.

How is that fair—especially when you compare it with times when you've thought, or even done, similar things yourself but God wouldn't let *you* get away with it? And, more to the point, how is that loving—to let somebody prosper at your expense?

You are not the first person to wrestle with this question. You're in good company with guys like Asaph, Job, and Habakkuk. What's more, you're in good company with God. Not only has he had his people address this good question multiple times, but he has preserved their wrestling in Scripture for thousands of years in order to help you.

For instance, consider what Asaph realizes in Psalm 73. Because wicked people don't experience consequences but only increase in wealth and power, their pride grows (see v. 6) and they reject any sense of having to give an account to God for their lives (see v. 11). They feel no remorse for what they've done and no need to turn to God for forgiveness.

This is their first taste of God's judgment. Their hearts get a little bit harder. They stay the course, unaware that they should live differently. They're on slippery footing without realizing that anything is wrong—and then, one day, they are utterly swept away (see vv. 18–20, 27).

God's present forbearance with them, as he allows them to hurt others—and maybe even to hurt you—is not a lack of goodness or power on his part. It's part of his judgment—a down payment now that promises a full reckoning later.

Here's how that truth helps you to have greater confidence in his love for you personally: If he doesn't let you get away with evil in your life, it's because he has something better for you. It shows that he thinks about you specifically and that he does so with good intentions, not with ruinous judgment. It shows that he loves you.

Reflect: Have there been times when you've doubted God's goodness or his power because someone hurt you and God seems to have let them get away with it?

Act: Think of times when God hasn't let you get away with evil. Thank him for loving you by pulling you up short and for wanting something better for you.

Act: Are there areas of evil that you've tucked away and tried not to deal with? Go to God now. Confess those areas. Ask him, in his mercy, to forgive you and to give you a soft heart that won't tolerate sin. Then let his love embrace you.

DAY 7

"I Don't Feel God's Presence Like I Once Did"

I bow my knees before the Father . . . that according to the riches of his glory he may grant you to be strengthened with power through his Spirit in your inner being, so that Christ may dwell in your hearts through faith—that you, being rooted and grounded in love, may have strength . . . to know the love of Christ that surpasses knowledge. (Eph. 3:14, 16–19)

HAVE YOU EVER found yourself thinking, "I just don't feel God's love or sense his presence like I used to"? If you were brave enough to tell a friend, they might have said something like "That's okay. Faith is not a feeling." I find that response unsatisfying—not only personally but also biblically.

Consider the Laodicean church (see Rev. 3:14–22). Jesus describes their actions as neither hot nor cold but lukewarm. This was so unappealing to him that he would have preferred them to be cold toward him instead. Their emotional response mattered to him. Their faith had a feeling.

Or think about the promise of 1 John 4:18: "perfect love casts out fear." Obviously fear is more than a mental construct or an act of the will. It's also an emotional response. Whatever drives it out must also be more than a mental construct or a willful act. Love, then, must be experienced even more than the fear it counteracts. Faith is not a feeling, but it has attendant feelings.

Look again at Ephesians 3:16–19. Notice how Paul knows that we have to experience our faith, not just think about it or act on it. He prays that our spirits will be strengthened to know Christ's love. And that knowing is much more than an intellectual, fact-based kind of knowledge. It's experiential. It's a knowing that surpasses knowledge. It's a connection with Christ that so fills you that you can't help but sense how much he loves you.

Clearly faith is more than a feeling, and it is possible to overemphasize the role that feelings play in your faith—but it is just as easy to undervalue them, as well.

What is one indicator, then, that you have really been saved—that you've been brought into a vital relationship with Christ? It's that you, having once had feelings of closeness with Christ, now want them again. When you feel like you're missing out on something with him, that is evidence that a relationship exists between you—a connection that gives you confidence to pursue him.

And it tells you more. That nagging sense of wanting more connection isn't one-sided. Your relationship with God is like any healthy relationship, in which both parties want to connect with each other. That dissatisfaction comes not only from you but also from the God who started a relationship with you. His Spirit yearns for more of you—even more than you do for him (see James 4:5).

Far from being a sign that you're not connected to God, being dissatisfied with his absence indicates that you already are connected to him and that he's calling you to have even more of him.

Reflect: Have you let yourself settle for an emotionless faith, out of the belief that it's okay to feel distant from God? If so, do you know why you have done so?

Reflect: Consider what it means that God longs jealously for the spirit he put within you.

Act: Do you want to feel more connected to this God? Do you believe that he wants that even more than you do? If that's true, then use Paul's prayer to ask Christ to dwell in your heart until you know the greatness of his love for you.

DAY 8

"Wrestling with Sin Shouldn't Be This Hard, Should It?"

In the days of his flesh, Jesus offered up prayers and supplications, with loud cries and tears, to him who was able to save him from death, and he was heard because of his reverence. Although he was a son, he learned obedience through what he suffered. (Heb. 5:7–8)

THE CHRISTIAN LIFE doesn't feel easy. It can be such a struggle to pursue Christ, live obediently, fight temptation, and engage a broken world with confident optimism. On good days, it can feel like you're barely standing in place. On bad days, it feels like everything is set against you, determined to keep you from living a godly life. It's exhausting. Wearing. And never-ending.

Not following Christ was so much easier—not better, but definitely easier. You did what you wanted, and evil didn't try to get in the way. It was like walking downhill. Sure, there were challenges, and the results were pretty stinky; but by comparison, it was a lot easier than following Jesus.

And that confuses people. They wonder, "How come life is so hard if I'm really saved? What am I doing wrong? What am I missing?" Instead of recognizing that it's harder to live now that the world, the flesh, and the devil are on the offensive in ways that they weren't previously (see Eph. 2:1–3), people start looking for the "key" that will open the lock of the Christian life. That's a fruitless search that will only end up wearing you out even more.

The reality is that in a fallen world, faith has never been easy for the people of God. That was true before Jesus came to earth, and it remains true afterward. Look no further than Peter and Paul—two of Jesus's most ardent followers—both of whom knew what it was to wrestle with their hearts . . . and lose (see Rom. 7:14–20; Gal. 2:11–14).

But don't stop there. Look at Jesus. Though human, he was still fully God (see John 1:1, 14). He was specially gifted with the Holy Spirit, he basked in his Father's approval (see Luke 3:22), and he had no doubt that his Father heard him when he prayed (see John 11:41–42). If anyone should have found the life of faith easy, it was Jesus. But he didn't.

The author of Hebrews is clear: Jesus learned to obey in the school of suffering. Living faithfully was so hard that he could do it only with loud cries and tears (see Heb. 5:7–8). Luke offers a glimpse into one of those moments in the garden of Gethsemane, when Jesus begged his Father for some future other than the cross (see Luke 22:39–44). He was in anguish, sweating profusely, struggling to stay faithful. And he did—but nothing about that wrestling was easy.

Struggling with sin and suffering is not a sign that God has abandoned you. It's normal for anyone who follows the Christ who worked so hard to stay faithful. The good news is that you'll never wrestle alone. Go to him. He's not surprised at how hard it is for you to live faithfully, and he will not turn you away when you ask for help (see Heb. 4:15–16).

Reflect: Has the difficulty of the Christian life surprised you? Has it worn you down?

Reflect: Meditate on how Jesus's struggle to stay faithful to God didn't harden him toward you but made him that much more sympathetic.

Act: Ask Jesus to give you the grace that you need—not merely to survive today's hardships but to grow even stronger in your faith and to move even closer to God.

DAY 9

"God Doesn't Answer My Prayers"

And [Jesus] said, "Abba, Father, all things are possible for you. Remove this cup from me. Yet not what I will, but what you will." (Mark 14:36)

SOMETIMES YOU LOSE confidence that God loves you because you've asked him to take something from you, or to give something to you, and he hasn't. And you can't figure out why. All that you want is one good friend—is that so much to ask?—or for your business to succeed, your chronic back pain to ease up, your ministry to take off, or your child to come back to the Lord. All good things to ask for—but he's not giving them to you.

You've done everything that you know to do. You've looked to see whether there's sin in your life. You've checked your heart for wrong motives. You can't think of anything wrong, but God is still not answering your prayer.

And so you start to lose heart. Clearly God is saying no—which your friends insist is an answer to your prayer, but it's an answer that doesn't make sense. You know that if someone asked you for the same thing, you would give it to them if you could. You can only conclude that something is wrong between you and God.

Or, at least, that's how you're responding to him now. You've pulled away. You talk to him less. You don't bother asking him for much anymore. You've lost confidence. You say you know that he loves you, but you're not acting like he does.

What's happened? You've evaluated God's love for you based on whether or not you've gotten what you wanted, and now you're not sure how strong that love is.

Did you know that Jesus didn't always get what he asked for? Three times he asked God if he could avoid the horrible suffering

33

of the cross (see Matt. 26:39, 42, 44). He didn't want it . . . but God said no to his Son—this Son whom God loved and with whom he was well-pleased (see Matt. 3:17; 17:5); who grew in favor with God over the course of his life (see Luke 2:52); who did only what he saw his Father doing (see John 5:19), because it was his food to do his Father's will (see John 4:34).

The reason that the Father said no had nothing to do with any fault in Jesus. Nor was there any fault in their relationship—Jesus had publicly prayed, "Father, I thank you that you have heard me. I knew that you always hear me" (John 11:41–42). He knew that his relationship with the Father was strong. He didn't evaluate it on the basis of what God gave or didn't give to him. Instead, he evaluated God's answer to his prayer based on what he knew of God's love for him. And so it didn't shake his confidence in God's love when God said no—even though that meant he would face the white-hot heat of God's wrath. Jesus was certain of the Father's love, because he knew the Father's heart.

You can be certain too. The Father has shown his heart to you by giving you his Son. If he gave his best to you without your asking him to, then all other things that he gives or doesn't give come from that same heart, as well.

Reflect: Is there something you've asked for that God has chosen not to give you? How has that answer affected your confidence in his love?

Reflect: God's *no* to Jesus made it possible for him to say *yes* to a relationship with you. How does that commitment to you transform the way that you hear him now when he says no?

DAY 10

"I Just Feel Like God Isn't Happy with Me"

I am not aware of anything against myself, but I am not thereby acquitted. It is the Lord who judges me. Therefore do not pronounce judgment before the time, before the Lord comes, who will bring to light the things now hidden in darkness and will disclose the purposes of the heart. (1 Cor. 4:4–5)

HAVE YOU NOTICED that you have less confidence in your relationship with God on days when you wake up feeling vaguely guilty? You can't put your finger on any one thing in particular, but there's this nagging sense that you've done something wrong and that God is frowning at you.

Paul would dismiss that feeling, because he knows how God operates. When God judges, he brings to light what is hidden and exposes the motives of the heart. In other words, he's specific. He exposes something that can be identified and linked back to an equally identifiable cause. And Paul is confident that God is much better at identifying and judging those things than he himself is (see 1 Cor. 4:3–4).

Jesus said something similar when he described how the Holy Spirit would convict the world of sin, righteousness, and judgment (see John 16:8–11). When wickedness is involved, God does not bring a generalized feeling that something's wrong. He brings conviction.

And that only makes sense. If you bring a charge against someone in court, it has to be specific. You can't accuse someone of being "a bad person." They might be—but that's a summary of their character based on individual things they have done. Charges are not a character assessment; they're specific allegations. Why would God have a lower standard of specificity than we do?

Think about the cross. The wrath of God that Jesus endured on your behalf was not a generalized wrath. God directed specific wrath against Christ for specific things that you would do against him and his holiness. To absolve you of those things, Jesus paid the exact penalty that was generated by each particular evil that God identified and judged.

In other words, it's not your job to convict yourself of sin. It's God's. And that's a good thing, because you'd be horrible at it. None of us is very good at being good, which means that we're not good at identifying where we are bad or the extent of our badness. Our spiritual blindness and our inexperience with true goodness mean that human judgment is superficial at best. If it were up to us, we would identify far too few things as sin and would assess far too small a penalty for them. The resulting payment would be inadequate, leaving us still separated from God.

Thankfully, God examines and reveals your heart to you . . . which would be terrifying if he hadn't also taken the responsibility of paying for everything that he convicts you of.

Your role is to be open and sensitive to his Spirit. When he convicts you, repent. His conviction will be specific, which allows you to ask for specific forgiveness. When you're just feeling uneasy, you can confidently push that feeling aside as you trust God to do his job.

Act: Is there something that God is clearly putting his finger on in your life? If so, then ask his forgiveness just as clearly.

Act: If there's nothing explicitly wrong in your life but you feel vaguely guilty, ask God to either make clear what you've done wrong or give you greater trust that he will do so when something stands between the two of you.

DAY 11

"I Am No Good in My Eyes
or Anyone Else's"

*"But a Samaritan, as he journeyed, came to where he was, and
when he saw him, he had compassion." (Luke 10:33)*

HAVE YOU EVER felt like eyes were all around, watching you?
Eyes that silently waited for the next time you slipped up, messed
up, or didn't measure up. Eyes that gave you a haunted, hunted
feeling. Eyes that saw you with judgment.

Or maybe they haven't always been other people's eyes.
Maybe at times they have been your own. When you have been
viewed with judgment, sometimes that way of looking finds a
home inside your own heart and mind. You routinely look for
the negatives in what you have thought and done, and you find
them. You regularly second-guess yourself and your motives and
are prepared to believe the worst about yourself. You internalize
other people's criticism until it becomes the lens through which
you view your own life.

When that happens, it's a short step to take to assume that this
must be how God sees you, too. It just makes sense that he can see
every flaw and fault that you can; and if you don't like what you
see, he couldn't possibly. At the least, he's got to be deeply disappointed in you. More likely, he's fed up—right?

Hearing that God loves you won't mean much if you're convinced that he's frustrated and critical, wondering when you'll
get your act together—wondering *if* you'll get it together. Little
will torpedo your confidence in his love faster or more effectively
than believing that he sees you with judgment.

Maybe that's why Scripture shows you a God who sees

people with a compassion so strong that it compels him to help them. Hagar discovers that he's the seeing God who cares about her in her misery (see Gen. 16:11–13). Moses learns that God is so moved by seeing the Israelites' misery that he plans to rescue them (see Ex. 3:7-8). And Jesus, God made flesh, embodied this same combination of traits as he walked on earth. He saw the helpless state of the crowds that flocked to him and had compassion on them, teaching and healing them (see Matt. 9:35–36; 14:14). He was deeply moved when he saw his friend Mary weeping, and he acted to set right what was wrong (see John 11:33).

These aspects of God's character are so important that Jesus built them into his parables. A Samaritan helps a man who's been beaten, because he sees him and is filled with compassion (see Luke 10:33). A father runs to greet his wayward child because he is moved with compassion when he sees him return home (see Luke 15:20).

God sees you with compassion. It's who he is. When you've lost confidence in him and believe that he sees you with judgment, you need to remind yourself, "No—he sees me with compassion." When you cringe and are waiting for someone to rebuke you for what you've said or done, remind yourself, "He sees me with compassion." When that feeling of dread steals over your heart, remind yourself, "He sees me with compassion." When you're afraid that you are about to be found out for the fraud that you think you are, remind yourself, "He sees me with compassion."

Repeat it to yourself—not as a mantra to empty your mind, but as the truth that must fill your soul.

Reflect: In what situations or circumstances do you most need to be reminded of how God sees you?

Act: Look up the passages above and notice how tightly God's compassion is tied to his seeing.

DAY 12

"I Just Know That God
Is Upset with Me"

*By this we shall know that we are of the truth and reassure our heart
before him; for whenever our heart condemns us, God is greater
than our heart, and he knows everything. (1 John 3:19–20)*

HAVE YOU EVER argued with yourself after sinning, only to find
that you couldn't win? A voice inside you takes the role of prosecutor: "I can't believe you did that. How could you even think
of something like that? You know better. That was so disgusting.
You're disgusting. God could never love you. No one could."

You try to mount a defense, but since all the evidence favors
the prosecution, you just come off sounding defensive. "It wasn't
like that. I mean, it wasn't that bad. Not as bad as you make it
sound. There were other factors involved—extenuating circumstances. Anybody else in my place would have done the same
thing."

Your best arguments sound weak, even to your own ears. You
can keep piling up hollow objections, but it won't be enough to
counter the solid accusations—and your heart knows it. It sides
with the prosecution and condemns you. Your defense falters,
because you know that your heart is right. The conclusion, then,
seems valid: God couldn't possibly keep loving someone like you.

Trying to prove to yourself that you're good enough for God
to love is always a losing proposition. It's doomed to fail, because
a flawed assumption that's built into it renders it impotent: the
assumption that you can produce some version of righteousness
that adequately approaches God's. You're trying to prove the
impossible. The data is stacked against you.

That's when you need to drop out of the argument by admitting, again, that you never had the kind of goodness that got you any credit with God (see Isa. 64:6–7; Rom. 3:9–20). If you weren't good enough before you first met God, why bother debating the virtues of your goodness now?

Instead, go back to what is true: God is greater than your heart (see 1 John 3:20). He knows the depths of your ugliness far more than any internal accusing voice does. He's seen it more clearly, and been far more affronted by it, than you—with your human limitations and sin-deceived soul—can begin to imagine. He knows everything. And he wanted you anyway.

And so Jesus came to silence the prosecution—not by bolstering your defense or by pretending that your sin doesn't matter, but by paying all the penalties for your sin that God's justice demands.

The worst that the prosecution can ever do is make you feel bad, and there are times when your heart will go along and willingly condemn you. Be at peace—God is still greater than your heart. He can free you from the guilt you feel so keenly so that your heart can rest in his presence.

Reflect: What are the favorite lines that your inner prosecutor repeatedly uses against you?

Reflect: Have you ever been able to fully set your heart at rest by arguing against it when it condemns you? If not, why would you keep trying?

Act: Pay attention to your heart today. For each time that it condemns you, remind yourself three times how much greater God is—that he knows everything you've ever done and wanted you anyway.

DAY 13

"Have I Done Enough to Be Saved?"

[Christ] entered once for all into the holy places, not by means
of the blood of goats and calves but by means of his own blood,
thus securing an eternal redemption. (Heb. 9:12)

HAVE YOU EVER wondered, "When I asked God to forgive me, was I truly sincere? Did I really repent? Did I confess all my sins? Was I specific enough? Comprehensive enough? Sorry enough?"

You may not realize it, but those questions are a sneaky version of *works righteousness*. That's how theologians describe any attempt to say to God, "I've been good enough for you, and so you should save me."

Are you surprised that repenting can become a "work"? Most religious activities can. You fall into this trap any time you make gaining God's mercy contingent on your own efforts—such as asking for forgiveness "the right way" or being remorseful "enough." Thankfully, God addressed this version of works righteousness thousands of years ago.

In the Old Testament, God foreshadowed what Jesus would do on the cross by telling his people to offer an animal sacrifice as a substitute death on their behalf. The animal would symbolically take the penalty for the human's sin on itself and would die, rather than the person who had sinned.

Even before God established the tabernacle or the temple, he told his people that they could make an earthen or stone altar on which to offer their sacrifices (see Ex. 20:24–26). But he gave them explicit instructions not to shape or cut the stones (see v. 25). They had to use them as they found them. This didn't simply distinguish the appearance of their altars from those of their surrounding neighbors. It clarified the role that his people played in atoning for their sin: none at all. They didn't create or give life to the creatures that they sacrificed, nor did they create the materials that were used to sacrifice them. They couldn't even set their own stamp on those materials.

The altar pictured the mind-set that the people needed to approach God. It was a mind-set that said, "I have no part in fixing the problem I have created between God and me. All that I bring to this altar is my sin. The only reason I don't die for my sin, as God's presence comes near, is that he has offered to accept a substitute for me. If he's satisfied with the sacrifice, then I live. If he isn't, then there's nothing I can do to satisfy him."

It was never a matter of doing enough, because there was never anything you could do. By asking, "Did I do enough? Well enough?" you're really asking, "Is God satisfied with what I've done?" The question that you need to ask instead is "Is God satisfied with what Christ has done?"

Since Jesus entered the Most Holy Place—and not an earthly copy of heaven's throne room, but the real one in which God's presence dwells (see Heb. 9:24–26)—then the answer throughout Scripture and heaven to "Is God satisfied?" is a resounding "Yes! It is enough."

Let that answer resound in your heart just as loudly.

Reflect: Consider what is the underlying root of your question "Did I repent well enough?" Does that question come from (1) wanting to think well of yourself, (2) hating to be in another's debt, (3) not wanting to feel vulnerable, (4) wanting to feel in control of your life, or (5) wanting to show God that you really do care? Or does it come from something else entirely?

Act: Here's the good news: even for this, Jesus's sacrifice was enough. Ask him to forgive you, and then rejoice in the greatness of his salvation.

DAY 14

"I See More and More Sin Every Time I Look"

I said: "Woe is me! For I am lost; for I am a man of unclean lips, and I dwell in the midst of a people of unclean lips; for my eyes have seen the King, the LORD of hosts!" (Isa. 6:5)

WHEN MANY PEOPLE start to follow Christ, they see a few things in their lives that need to be straightened out—things they have tried to deal with or even things that they've resisted admitting were a problem. Once the Spirit of God breaks through, they can finally confess their sins, feel forgiven, and be filled with joy.

They then throw themselves into the life of the church, learning, growing, and sharing . . . but, over time, something unexpected happens. They start to discover areas of weakness or stubbornness that they didn't know they had. Their Scripture-reading convicts them of something they had thought was okay. They hear their small-group leader or pastor talk about something that they never considered to be a problem. They rub shoulders with people who have walked with Christ for a long time, people who exude real kindness and gentleness and compassion and courage, and they're embarrassed by their own lack of these qualities. It's strange—being with God and his people starts to make them feel like they're becoming worse, not better.

Ever felt like that? As weird as that is, it's normal.

As you come closer to holiness, your wickedness becomes more obvious. That's true not just for you and me, but for all God's people.

When Isaiah—one of God's greatest prophets—saw God, he immediately concluded that he was so unholy that he had no hope. Seeing God did not produce sin in Isaiah. It showed him the ugliness of what was already there. Despite being a prophet—one who took God's words on his lips—he confessed that his lips were unclean. But he had previously had no idea of this.

Hear this the right way, and it will set you free: you also have no idea. You haven't begun to see the least part of your problem. And I haven't, either. I'm still on the front end of seeing my participation in evil for what it is. I now see whole new depths of things in me that are repulsive. Things that God has always been aware of but that I have not.

How is that helpful? It's helpful because the God who has always seen clearly has already crafted a solution that meets all our needs at every level. It's the altar that stands before him (see Isa. 6:6). More specifically, it's the sacrifice on the altar. That sacrifice, which anticipates Christ offering himself on the cross, doesn't merely purify the flawed prophet's lips but transforms them so that they can proclaim the message of the King (see Isa. 6:6–8).

Spend time in that King's presence, and you'll see your unrighteousness more clearly. At times you will feel like you are lost. But look beyond yourself to him, and you'll see his forward-looking grace both anticipating and meeting your need.

Yes, mourn your failings; but go beyond them, as well, and celebrate his proactive response to them—a response that lets you stand joyfully in his presence.

Reflect: If God doesn't expect you to pay for your sin or want you to be crushed by it, why does he show you more of it? Are you moved yet to celebrate his desire to free you from it?

Act: The next time your failures threaten to demoralize you, remind yourself that God has already provided in Christ everything that you need to be cleansed from the sin that you now see and from all that you ever will see.

FINDING CERTAINTY IN GOD'S FAITHFUL ACTS

DAY 15

Jesus Says, "I Have Prayed for You"

*"Simon, Simon, behold, Satan demanded to have you,
that he might sift you like wheat, but I have prayed for you
that your faith may not fail. And when you have turned
again, strengthen your brothers." (Luke 22:31–32)*

WHEN DO YOU lose confidence in your friendships? Isn't it most often when you realize that people can't handle you in your weaker moments?

If a relationship falters because of something you did—because you let the other person down, didn't carry through on a promise, said something inappropriate, or even sinned against them—then you learn that the friendship is only as good or as strong as you are. When that happens, you lose confidence in the other person's commitment to you.

Conversely, if they can handle you well when you're not at your best, then you grow more confident in them and in your relationship with them.

Watch, then, as Jesus engages Peter at one of Peter's least impressive moments. Jesus was eating the Passover meal with his disciples on the night he was betrayed. He knew that they would all abandon him (see Matt. 26:31). In a few short hours they would all be faithless, and Peter would lead the charge as he denied even knowing Christ (see Matt. 26:34).

Remember that this is the guy who confessed earlier that Jesus was God's Messiah—the one who would save his people (see Matt. 16:16). Put yourself in his place. Can you imagine the uncertainty that would flood your mind after you had rejected him? How you'd wonder whether someone who could deny the Savior had ever really been saved—or, worse, now that you'd distanced yourself from him, *could* ever be saved? Wouldn't you end up wondering, "What hope is there for me now?"

The hope was there before Peter even sinned. Jesus told him that he knew what Peter would do before he did it. His faithless denial didn't surprise Jesus. More importantly, Jesus told him what he had already done for him in advance. He prayed that Peter's faith wouldn't fail and that he would turn back—that he would have more confidence in Christ's ability to save him than in his own ability to place himself beyond salvation.

This same Jesus now prays for you (see Heb. 7:25). If he prays for people's faith not to fail in extreme cases, don't you think that he also prays for your faith not to fail as you question his love for you or his ability to save you?

The only difference is that he no longer prays on earth with his glory cloaked; now, having been raised from the dead and exalted to the right hand of God, he prays in heaven, where he is radiant and glorified beyond our imagining (see Rom. 8:34; Heb. 1:3).

His prayer was powerfully effective on earth. What possible reason could you have for believing that it's less so now?

Reflect: Have you noticed that Jesus is not intimidated by his people's struggles with faith?

Reflect: Do you see how proactively Christ works right now to rescue people from themselves?

Act: Take a few minutes and thank him for all the ways he is continuing to work in your life to bring you closer to himself.

DAY 16

Jesus Says, "I Will Never Drive Away the One Who Comes to Me"

"All that the Father gives me will come to me, and whoever comes to me I will never cast out." (John 6:37)

A WOMAN ONCE jokingly told me—at least I think it was a joke—"I don't want to be cremated because, just in case I don't make it [to heaven], I don't want to burn twice."

We laughed it off—but what was she saying, underneath the dark humor? Something in the back of her mind was asking, "What if, after loving and serving Jesus for decades, I find out I was fooling myself—but I only realize that when I wake up in hell?"

It's no secret that you can follow Jesus for all the wrong reasons—reasons that have nothing to do with him. A large crowd once did (see John 6:22–24). They made a special trip across a lake just to see him, but they didn't expend all that effort because they wanted *him*. They wanted what he could do for them. They saw him as their meal ticket (see John 6:26, 30–31, 34) but didn't realize that this was what they were doing.

That story might leave you unsure regarding your own motives for following Jesus. But God doesn't want you to be unsure. Neither did he want the crowd to be uncertain. So Jesus explained to them how you can know that you aren't fooling yourself. He said that those whom the Father gives him will come to him; that those who come will never be driven away; that the Father is determined that Jesus lose none of those he has been given; that, instead of allowing them to be lost, Jesus will raise them up to eternal life (see vv. 37–40). Unfortunately, as you keep reading, you learn that many in the crowd left him—thereby demonstrating that they were not those whom the Father had given to him (see v. 66).

But not everyone left. The twelve apostles stayed (see vv. 68–69).

At least, they all stayed for a time. Judas would later leave, as Jesus predicted (see vv. 70–71)—indicating that he too was interested in Jesus only for what he could get out of him. For him, as for the crowd, Jesus was a means to an end, not the most glorious end in himself.

In other words, if you're interested in Christ because you can't imagine a life without him, then you don't need to fear hell. No one in hell says, "I was kind of afraid that this would happen, but I was hoping things would turn out differently because all I ever really wanted was Jesus." Those who choose an eternity away from God may long for comfort, but they don't long for God (see Luke 16:19–24).

So what happens if you discover that, like the crowd or like Judas, you are trying to use Jesus? Well, does this bother you? Does it upset you to see this about yourself? If it does, it means that what you really want *is* him. And that means that you can confess the sin of how you were trying to use him, and can know that one day he will raise you up from that transgression as well as from all the others.

Reflect: Ask yourself, "If I was forced to give everything up that I hold dear, would Jesus be the last thing I let go of?"

Act: If nothing else is more special to you than Jesus, then rejoice that the Father has given you to him. And if you wish that he was more special to you than he is, ask his forgiveness, trust his power to save you from yourself, and then rejoice!

DAY 17

God Does Not Treat You as Your Doubt Deserves

*Then [Jesus] said to Thomas, "Put your finger here, and
see my hands; and put out your hand, and place it in my
side. Do not disbelieve, but believe." (John 20:27)*

SOME PASSAGES IN the Bible make doubt sound like the sin
that God will not pardon. James declares that if you want wisdom
from God, you must "ask in faith, with no doubting" (James 1:6).
The author of Hebrews tells you that "without faith it is impossible to please [God]" (Heb. 11:6).

What does that mean, then, if you are wrestling with thoughts
such as "I don't know if God likes me. I don't know if I am one of
his children. I really want to be his child, but I'm not sure that I'm
one of the elect. I don't know if I'm really saved"? Those thoughts
kind of sound like doubt, right? So does this all mean that God
is not pleased with you and that you really don't belong to him?

Let's come at it from a different direction—let's start with
God and his character before we get to you and your thoughts.
Remember Thomas, one of Jesus's disciples? He wasn't around
when Jesus first appeared to his followers after his death, and so
Thomas declared that he just couldn't believe that Jesus was alive.

Jesus didn't get angry with him or keep his distance. Rather,
he moved toward Thomas, appearing again when Thomas was
present and going straight to him—not to lecture Thomas, berate
him, belittle him, or even remind him of all that he had said
about rising again after being killed. Instead, he offered him the
proof that Thomas needed in order to believe. Jesus bent himself
around the doubter's needs. Do you see how he is comfortable

around doubters, and yet doesn't leave them to flail about in their uncertainty? He doesn't treat them as their doubt deserves, but he nurtures their souls and leads them from unbelief to faith.

So when you read passages like the ones from James and Hebrews above, read them through the filter of what God is like. He isn't shocked at, appalled at, surprised by, dismayed by, or scared of your doubts. Instead, he has anticipated them. He expected doubt to be a real problem for many of his people, and he did something about it. He talked openly about your struggles with doubt and wrote down what you need to do.

And he did that thousands of years before you even knew that you had a problem. Far from being intimidated by your struggle or disappointed in you, he gives you the help you need in order to get beyond that struggle and to be more certain of his love for you.

The passages in the Bible about doubt are evidence of the heart he has for doubters—a heart that longs to strengthen your faith and end your doubt. They're not there to give you less confidence in him; they're there to give you more.

Reflect: What do you learn about God's heart for doubters from the way he talks about doubt and how to overcome it? Have you ever thanked him for caring so much about the things that you struggle with?

Act: Are you used to thinking of God as someone who cares about doubters and about what they need in order to believe and trust him? What do you need from him that will give you confidence in his love for you? Ask him for it.

DAY 18

You Didn't Conceive Yourself

But to all who did receive him, who believed in his name, he gave the
right to become children of God, who were born, not of blood nor of the
will of the flesh nor of the will of man, but of God. (John 1:12–13)

YOU DIDN'T CHOOSE to be born. That's one of the most obvious truths about every member of the human race. You didn't
conceive you. You didn't carry you or labor for you. You didn't
birth you. You're alive, and yet you owe nothing of that life to
yourself. Birth happened to you because of other people's actions
and consequent decisions. Otherwise you wouldn't be here.

John uses what we know of human birth—that it has nothing
to do with the baby—in order to help us understand spiritual
birth. Spiritual life doesn't originate in the human race. It isn't
passed along to you by your relatives or connected to any deci-
sion or action that is made by anyone in the human race. It comes
from God.

You can no more decide that you want to be spiritually alive
than you can decide that you want to be physically alive. Physical
life first has to happen to you before you can then respond physically. Babies don't take their first breath and cry in order to be
alive; they breathe and cry because they already are.

Only those who are physically alive can respond to the world
around them. They're aware that they are alive. Those who are
dead are not only unresponsive to the world but also unaware of
their condition. It takes life in order to recognize the difference
between liveliness and deadness.

Now draw out the implications for your faith. Can you
remember a time when you realized that some people are spiritually alive while others are spiritually dead? Did it upset you that

you might not have spiritual life? Did your concern move you to come to God—to ask him to give you that life through faith in Jesus Christ? Have you continued to want that life? Does it still bother you when you worry that you might not be spiritually alive? Do those concerns move you to ask God for help? If so, then be at peace. Those are not the thoughts and actions of someone who is spiritually dead.

But how did you get that life? You didn't give it to yourself. God gave it to you. He conceived you and carried you until he birthed you. As much as you may have wrestled with deciding whether or not to follow Christ, he first gave you the life that made your wrestling and decision-making possible.

And that's great news. If spiritual life comes from him and not from you or from anything you have done, then you don't need to worry about losing it. You can't. He decided to birth you; you didn't decide to be born.

It gets better. God doesn't abandon or ignore the children whom he brings to life. Since it was his choice to add you to his family, you can trust him to parent you in such a way that you will be with him forever.

Reflect: Have you given much thought to John's analogy between physical and spiritual birth? What other aspects of your spiritual life does this metaphor illuminate that are helpful to you?

Act: Realizing that you had no role in your own spiritual birth ends up giving you greater confidence in God's love for you—but it is a humbling thing to accept. Take some time to talk with God about where your heart is as far as embracing or resisting that reality.

DAY 19

You Didn't Resurrect Yourself

God, being rich in mercy, because of the great love with which he loved
us, even when we were dead in our trespasses, made us alive together
with Christ—by grace you have been saved—and raised us up with
him and seated us with him in the heavenly places in Christ Jesus,
so that in the coming ages he might show the immeasurable riches
of his grace in kindness toward us in Christ Jesus. (Eph. 2:4–7)

WHAT IS THE essence of assurance? It's knowing not simply that God loves you now but also that he won't stop loving
you—that you can't lose his love. One way to grow more confident, more assured, of his love is to think about the nature of
existence—about what it means to be alive.

Being bounded by time gives us a funny perspective on life
and death. We think of death as an ending—and as an ending
that is far more final than it actually is. And because we think that
death ends life, we misunderstand its limitations. Death ends life
only here on earth; think for a moment, and you'll realize that
even after it ends here, life itself keeps going (see Dan. 12:2; Matt.
25:46; John 5:29). Existence is eternal.

Everyone enters into an endless, ongoing existence that they
cannot lose, regardless of their death on earth. Accidents can take
their physical life, disease can take it, others can take it, age can
take it, and they themselves can take it, but none of those things
actually ends their life. Even if they die without knowing God,
they will continue existing—although, to be fair, it might be better to call it a living death.

But those who know God have been raised out of that living
death so that their spirits, which were once dead, are now alive
(see Eph. 2:5). And I trust that, since you are reading this book,

this is you—or at least that you want it to be you—otherwise this book would hold no interest for you.

Christian, you are one whom God raised to life. Previously you had no life—at least none that counted with God. You were dead in your sins. But God loved you so much that he gave you life. You didn't choose to give yourself life. You didn't have the power or the ability to do so.

Now use what you understand about the visible creation to help you understand the spirit world that's invisible. In the same way that your physical existence can't be taken from you once it's been given, your spiritual life can't either. You didn't have the power or ability to grant yourself that life, nor do you have the power or ability to take it from yourself. And neither does anyone else.

Take it one step further. God chose to give you that endless spiritual life so that you would be with him. And while you are with him, he intends to show you the rich kindness of his grace (see Eph. 2:7). How long do you think it will take to work through those immeasurable riches?

An immeasurable amount of time seems like a reasonable estimate.

In other words, having loved you to life, he plans to love you forever.

Reflect: Have you fallen into the trap of giving physical death more credit than it deserves?

Reflect: How strongly do you see the connection between God's love and your being alive spiritually?

Act: If you have experienced being spiritually alive, then thank God for loving you both now and forever. If you haven't yet, what is keeping you from asking to be loved? Remember that he has promised never to turn away anyone who comes to him (see John 6:37).

DAY 20

You Didn't Start Loving God
before He Loved You

*In this is love, not that we have loved God but that he loved us and
sent his Son to be the propitiation for our sins. (1 John 4:10)*

IT'S EASY TO generate doubt by taking a good aspect of your
relationship with God and overinflating its importance. For
instance, it is very important to examine your love for God by
asking if he is your greatest treasure (see Matt. 13:45–46). But if
that examination focuses on the quality of your own love without
reference to God's, you will tend to see him as passive—as the
one who is loved and adored—while you take center stage as the
more active partner.

That error will lead you to emphasize your love for him over
his love for you, at which point you will erode whatever assurance you once had in his love. You will inevitably feel insecure in
the relationship, because your love will never be as committed,
dependable, constant, enduring, and unwavering as would befit
this great God.

That doesn't mean that your love is irrelevant. It matters
greatly. But it matters secondarily. It's your response to him. If
you forget the primacy of his love in initiating, undergirding, surrounding, and nourishing your relationship, you will inevitably
focus on how well you are loving him.

But you already know how unsteady your heart is. How long
can you watch your passion fluctuate before wondering when
God will decide that you're too fickle and that he's no longer
interested?

That's when you need the grace of being reminded that love

has a source outside yourself. It comes from God (see 1 John 4:7). We can love like God does only because he loved us before we loved him or anyone else (see 1 John 4:10, 19). He never based the strength of his love for you on the strength of yours for him. He knew that you needed to be loved in order to love.

If you see any inclination in yourself to love him, that's an effect of his love—an indication that he already loves you. And that's reassuring. Does your love for him seem weak and feeble at times? Try looking at it from a different perspective: Do you have any love at all? Since you used to have none, the presence of some tells you that right now, he loves you.

And if you started with none but now have some, then you can have confidence that in the future you will have even more, because you know that he won't stop loving you. If Jesus loved you when you had nothing to offer and were completely unlovable, why would he love you less now that you can and do love him in return?

Reflect: Why do you suppose it's so easy to forget that God loved you first and to get more caught up in how good a job you're doing with loving him?

Reflect: What makes it hard for you to trust that Christ's love doesn't waver even when yours does?

Act: The apostle John puts things so simply and clearly in all his writings—and especially so in his first letter. Are there different ways that you can let his vocabulary sink more deeply into your mind and heart? Here's an example: read 1 John 4:7–12 out loud each day for a week, write out the passage and post it where you will see it regularly, and memorize key verses—or even memorize all of it.

DAY 21

Your Doubt Doesn't
Cause God to Doubt

*Jesus immediately reached out his hand and took hold of him, saying
to him, "O you of little faith, why did you doubt?" (Matt. 14:31)*

SOME OF US are quiet doubters. We're afraid to let anyone
know that we're not always sure whether God loves us or confident that he has brought us into his family. That's embarrassing to
admit—especially if you've been a Christian for a while.

You may have even helped other people to come to Christ or
grow in their faith, but here you are wondering, "Does he really
love me?" Who can you share that with? Other believers might
think less of you or not let you serve anymore. Or, worse, your
uncertainty might cause someone else to stumble.

The apostle Peter was different. He was one of those guys who
could live out his faith publicly—even when it was embarrassing.

Jesus had called him to be one of his apostles (see Luke
6:13–14). He wanted Peter to be with him, and he wanted to
send him out to preach (see Mark 3:14). Peter was part of Jesus's
inner circle, and he was also the first person to publicly declare
that Jesus was God's Messiah (see Matt. 16:15–20). But, not too
much earlier, his confidence in Christ had faltered.

He and the other disciples had been in a boat and were not
making much progress as they headed into a strong wind—
when Jesus walked out to them on the surface of the lake. Peter
asked Jesus to invite him to come to him on top of the waves, and
Jesus did.

Peter started well. He stepped out of the boat and began walking toward Jesus, but then he looked around and was overawed

at the power of the broken creation that opposed them, and he began to sink. Jesus rescued him, but also called him out, saying, "Why did you doubt?"

Jesus named the issue publicly, but not to shame Peter or embarrass him. Nor did that doubt follow him the rest of his life to affect his relationship with Christ or his ministry. Peter not only continued to be an apostle but also helped to lead the other apostles after Jesus ascended into heaven, and he was the vehicle through which Jesus turned many people from their sins to himself (see Acts 2:14–41).

Doubt did not forever define Peter or mark how Jesus related to him—it didn't discourage Jesus, back him off, or make him rethink his choice. Jesus put his finger on the problem so that Peter could move beyond it instead of staying stuck in it. Peter's doubt in God did not make God doubt his choice of Peter or his plans for Peter's life.

In the same way, your doubt in his love does not cause Jesus to doubt the wisdom of loving you. He doesn't believe that doubt will have the last word on you. You shouldn't either.

Reflect: Jesus loves you, regardless of your doubts. No doubt of yours will make him back away or disown you.

Act: Are you afraid of talking with God about your doubts? Ask him to show you how your doubt doesn't intimidate him or turn him against you. Ask him to show you instead how much he wants to free you from your doubt.

Act: Have you been afraid to tell other people your doubts? Ask God for a friend or mentor who can handle hearing what you're wrestling with and can help you to see that God is not afraid of your secret doubts.

DAY 22

God's Justice Removes Doubt

*If we confess our sins, he is faithful and just to forgive us our sins
and to cleanse us from all unrighteousness. (1 John 1:9)*

LET'S START FROM the beginning: you are made in the image
of God. Whenever someone sees you or interacts with you,
they're supposed to say to themselves, "That's the kind of thing
God would think or say or feel or do if he were standing here right
now."

That reality creates a problem, however—because every time
you live like God wouldn't, you misrepresent him. You proclaim
something about him that's not true, and you take away from his
glory. In order for the world to be set right, that deficit of glory
has to be filled in—your debt to his holiness has to be repaid.

Enter God's justice. His justice demands that the guilty make
reparations to any and all aggrieved parties—including himself.
If he did any less, he would no longer be fully just; he'd be allowing a wrong to go unrighted. And if that were the case, that flaw
in him—however small—would extend into his universe, ultimately becoming its undoing.

Do you see the dilemma? In order to visibly represent him,
God's images must be free from all glory-debts. How can he
remain perfectly, wonderfully, and gloriously just and still have
a relationship—let alone share eternity—with those who have
transgressed his holiness?

He can't say, "Oh, it doesn't matter," because it does—both
for his own character and for the whole of creation. He could
demand that the offenders pay back what they owe, but since
they've infringed infinite glory, it will take finite creatures an
infinite amount of time to repay.

Enter God's Son. If someone who could pay off an infinite amount of debt within the confines of finite time would willingly join himself to the guilty, then simultaneously their debt would be paid and God's justice would be completely satisfied. That's what Jesus was doing on the cross.

The cross is not a sentimental picture of love. It's a payment: what you once owed is owed no longer. And if it is no longer owed, then there's nothing to prevent God from loving you or to hinder you from coming to him to be loved.

Has anyone ever told you that "God treats you now just as if you hadn't sinned"? That's a bad way to describe what's going on. It's not fully true, and it sounds as if God is pretending—"Let's pretend that you're better than you are." Where's the assurance in that? If he treats you "as if" today, what's to keep him from treating you "not as if" tomorrow?

The cross is so much more robust. Jesus paid what you owe—your past sins, present sins, and future sins—so that God says, "You did sin; but when you joined yourself to my Son, your sin was exhaustively paid in full."

If that's the case, then it would be completely inappropriate and wrong—sinful, even—for God to demand, or even ask, that you pay any additional amount in any way. If he did, he would be unjust (see 1 John 1:9). Jesus didn't go through all that he did for you, didn't fully meet the demands of justice, so that you could now relate to an unjust God.

Reflect: If Jesus paid for not only your past sins but your entire lifetime sin-debt, what is left to keep God from loving you?

Act: Are there sins that you're afraid are blocking God's love? What will you do to focus yourself more on what Jesus did than on what you have done?

DAY 23

You Have Life Because God Breathes It into You

Then he said to me, "Prophesy to the breath; prophesy, son of man, and say to the breath, Thus says the Lord God*: Come from the four winds, O breath, and breathe on these slain, that they may live." So I prophesied as he commanded me, and the breath came into them, and they lived and stood on their feet, an exceedingly great army. (Ezek. 37:9–10)*

CONSIDER EZEKIEL'S GLIMPSE into a valley that was littered with bones—bones that had been there so long that they weren't simply dry; they were very dry (see Ezek. 37:2). Desiccated. Absolutely lifeless, and unable to do anything for themselves. After showing Ezekiel this, God asks him a ridiculous question: "Son of man, can these bones live?" Ezekiel answers brilliantly, putting the question back in God's lap: "O Lord God, you know" (v. 3).

So then God tells the prophet what future he has in mind for the bones—that they must live—and commands him to proclaim that future to the bones. Ezekiel stands back and watches as that future hope breaks in to the present reality. The bones come alive. They reconnect, linking together as they were commanded to do. Then they are clothed: muscles, tendons, cartilage, and skin cover over them—but something is missing. They look like people, but they have no life in them (see v. 8).

God is not content with the mere appearance of life. He tells the prophet to command breath to enter them, at which point they rise up on their feet. They become what previously they could not be: living persons. Fully complete images of God. Not inanimate mockeries of life, but robust human beings.

It's a second creation story. A re-creation. A New Creation. A reminder of when God formed humans from the dust of the earth and breathed life into them so that they became living creatures (see Gen. 2:7). Only this time he's not starting from simple dust. He's starting with the lifeless remains of people who are under the power of death. But when he is done, life replaces death. The spirit of God reverses the curse. They are revived. Resurrected.

But wait. Who are they? They are God's people—who, though physically alive, are alienated from him, living in exile because they had rejected him and his ways (see Ezek. 37:11–14). The very dry bones depict the utter helplessness and hopelessness of their spiritual condition. But God refuses to accept that condition, and so he breathes life into them so that they retake their place in his world.

That's what God does for people who have no hope. He revives them—*and* he wants them to know what he's doing, so he gives them a picture of hope. This picture underlines what you contribute to the work of being made spiritually alive: you bring death—death that is so utterly dead, it is anyone's guess whether you could ever live again or not. It underlines what God contributes by breathing life into you: he longed for you to live so badly that he sent his Spirit into you to turn his longing into reality. It underlines what is utterly absurd: to believe that there is anything in the universe that could kill you spiritually if he wants you alive. If death, as the last enemy, isn't strong enough to thwart his desire for you, then nothing else can either.

> **Reflect:** What pictures of your spiritual life rule your mind and heart? How do those pictures encourage you to believe or to doubt?
>
> **Reflect:** How does this picture shed light on God's commitment to re-create you?

DAY 24

You Don't Pursue God More
Than He Pursues You

"The sheep hear [the shepherd's] voice, and he calls his own sheep by name and leads them out. When he has brought out all his own, he goes before them, and the sheep follow him, for they know his voice." (John 10:3–4)

WHO PURSUES WHOM? Do you pursue God, or does he pursue you? If I listened to you talk about your relationship with God over the past few months, would I hear more about how he comes to you or about what you do to connect with him? If you are like me or my friends, I would probably hear more about what you've been doing. That makes sense, given that many of us have heard sermons, read books, attended seminars, and been discipled on how to have a satisfying personal relationship with Christ.

While there's nothing wrong with understanding our part in our relationship with Christ, when we focus on the mechanics of Bible study and prayer, we unintentionally communicate that we are far more active than he is. That what he did historically made it possible for us to have a relationship with him, but that now the primary responsibility is on us to develop it.

While it is no one's intent, this focus paints a picture of a reclusive God who waits to see how much effort we'll put in before deciding to reciprocate. That picture can start to chip away at your confidence in actually having a saving relationship with him.

Thankfully, Jesus doesn't talk like that. While he does remind us of what he has done for us, he also emphasizes what he is still doing: "My sheep know me; they listen to my voice" (see John 10:14, 27). Think about how his sheep know what he sounds like. Do you get a picture of untended sheep who feverishly scour the pasture and pen for hints of his voice? Who, left to themselves, are desperately trying to recall previous conversations with him so they can remember what he sounds like?

No. You get a picture of the shepherd coming to them and calling them by name—a picture of intimacy that is initiated by him and is dependent on his continued involvement with them. He spends time with them. He talks to them. They can pick out his voice and distinguish it from a stranger's, because he takes it on himself to familiarize them with his voice (see John 10:5). He knows them—but, equally importantly, he makes sure that they know him.

What is the payoff of knowing his voice? Those to whom the shepherd speaks are the ones to whom he gives eternal life (see John 10:28). They get to live forever with the One whose voice they know.

Don't leapfrog over the present moment into the future and ask, "Am I saved? Will I go to heaven?" Ask instead, "Am I listening? Do I want to hear the shepherd?" If you do, then set your heart at rest, because only Christ's sheep care about hearing his voice.

And if you want to hear his voice, then listen with confidence—because Jesus is more invested in talking to his people than we are in hearing what he has to say.

Reflect: If you told me about your relationship with God, would I hear that he was more active in pursuing you or vice versa?

Reflect: What do you think are some of the things that get in the way and make it hard for you to hear the shepherd's voice?

Act: How does Christ most often speak to you? Through Scripture? Through remembered songs? In prayer? By showing you the wonders of his creation? Ask him to help you listen as he speaks today.

You Didn't Lead Yourself to Christ

"No one can come to me unless the Father who sent me draws him. And I will raise him up on the last day." (John 6:44)

IT HURTS OUR pride and disturbs our notion of "free will," but Jesus is very clear: if you have any interest in him, it is only because the Father has first drawn you to him. If the Father hadn't stirred your heart, you would not be attracted to his Son.

You do have to respond by moving toward Christ—by listening to him, talking with him, obeying him, enjoying him—but your actions are secondary to the Father's. This order is so foundational to your confidence in your relationship with God that Jesus repeats himself, leaving no room for misunderstanding (see John 6:37, 44, 65). If the Father has drawn you, then you can be sure Christ has saved you.

The question, then, is not "How can I know that I'm saved?" but "How can I know that the Father has drawn me?" The answer is found in how you react to Jesus: do you move toward him or away from him?

Jesus told these things to a large crowd that had invested serious time and energy in pursuing him (see John 6:22–24). But it turned out that they didn't want him as much as they wanted him to make their lives easier. They wanted a free lunch (see v. 26).

Jesus started dialoguing with them, challenging why they were following him so that they could want him for the right reasons. But the people wouldn't let go of what they wanted, which meant that they became more confused the longer he talked.

Jesus told them that they needed a different kind of food than the kind they were thinking about. They needed bread from heaven. Then he told them that he was that bread and that they would need to eat his flesh and drink his blood if they wanted to have real life (see vv. 32–33, 48–51, 53–58).

This didn't make any sense to them. A number of them walked away—including some who had considered themselves his disciples (see v. 66). But the twelve apostles didn't walk. When Jesus asked them if they wanted to, they told Jesus that they had nowhere else to go, because he alone had the words of life (see vv. 68–69).

It's pretty obvious that they didn't fully grasp what he was saying until after his resurrection, but they didn't let their confusion get in the way of pursuing him. Just the opposite—when they were confused about something that he said or did, they asked him about it (see Matt. 13:10; 15:12; Mark 7:17; 9:28; 13:1–4; Luke 8:9; John 11:7–15; 13:24–25, 36–37). They moved closer to him. They came to him and kept on coming to him and stayed with him, because they knew he was the Holy One of God (see John 6:69).

That's the key to understanding whether or not the Father has drawn you: do you critique and dismiss Jesus, or do you trust and want more of him? Neither the crowd nor the apostles fully understood what he was saying that day, but those whom the Father drew wanted more of him and wouldn't leave.

Reflect: Have there been times when you were tempted to walk away from Christ but didn't? What kept you from leaving?

Reflect: Has the Father drawn you to his Son? Do you still want Jesus? Are you still pursuing him?

Act: If the Father is continuing to draw you, take a moment and thank him for doing so.

PUTTING FINAL DOUBTS TO REST

DAY 26

"But How Do I Know I'm Part of God's Family?"

Because you are sons, God has sent the Spirit of his Son into our hearts, crying, "Abba! Father!" (Gal. 4:6)

IN GALATIANS 3:23–4:7, Paul wrestles with the question "Who inherits the promises given to Abraham of an eternal life with God?" Or, in our modern vernacular, who is saved?

The answer is everyone who trusts God to justify them through Christ's death and resurrection. All who believe—who take God at his word—regardless of their gender, social standing, or ethnicity, are now "sons" of God. This means that all who believe inherit equally. There are no second-class family members seated around God's dining room table.

But how do you know if you have a seat? The acid test of sonship comes from something inside you that insists—demands—that you think of God as your Father. It's the Spirit of his Son that he has sent into your heart that says, "You are related to him." Even in your worst moments, you know that you can turn to him and he will hear you, because you're family. And so you don't even think about it. You just expect him to take your call, because that's what family does.

This is an experiential argument, not a conceptual one. It asks you whether you find yourself naturally, if unexpectedly, turning to God in random moments of your life.

- Do you ever feel grateful and silently whisper, "Thank you"?
- Do you ever get upset and tell God how frustrated you are?
- Have you ever been sick or in pain and asked him to heal you?

71

- Have you ever urged him to make the future turn out a certain way?
- Have you ever felt cut to the heart and asked him to comfort you?
- Do you ever find yourself struck by the beauty of a sunset, the delicacy of a spiderweb, the power of a thunderstorm, the quietness of a snowfall, the softness of a baby's cheek, or the loyalty of a pet, and then find yourself marveling at the One who made it?

Responses like these—reaching out to God or associating him with the things you experience in life—make sense only if there is something real between the two of you. Something that transcends your fears and uncertainty. Something that's there whether you consciously think about it or not.

When you instinctively turn to God—not to make all your wishes come true, but in order to invite him into your world or to share yourself with him—you are demonstrating that his Spirit really is inside of you crying out, "Father!" It's the evidence that you are family.

Being family wasn't your idea first. God put the Spirit of his Son in you. And since he has done that, you are not just family for the moment—you are family forever.

Reflect: Think back over the past few days. Were there times when you casually, instinctively reached out to God?

Act: Be honest with yourself: do you have a sense inside that you can talk to God as your Father? If so, thank him for his Spirit. If not, ask him to adopt you and give you his Spirit.

DAY 27

What Is Most True of You Is What You Will One Day Only Be

I give thanks to my God always for you because of the grace of God that was given you in Christ Jesus . . . who will sustain you to the end, guiltless in the day of our Lord Jesus Christ. God is faithful, by whom you were called into the fellowship of his Son, Jesus Christ our Lord. (1 Cor. 1:4, 8–9)

A WOMAN ONCE told my friend, "I feel like God never really accepted me to begin with, because I'm so evil." You may not go as far as to say this same thing, but you may have felt the weight of its logic. Here's a foolproof way to make this happen: simply meditate on the wrong things. Turn over and over in your mind the list of foolish, sinful things that you regret having done. Itemize them carefully to make sure that none are missing, then relive each painful detail—and guess what? You'll feel shame and embarrassment much more keenly than you'll feel God's love.

Those feelings of guilt and distance from God come when you mistakenly believe that your destiny is controlled primarily by what you have done in the past and the present. And it isn't.

What determines your future is Jesus's past and present. He already, in his life and death, earned perfect righteousness that he then traded with you in order to take on your wickedness and every penalty associated with it (see Rom. 3:21–22; 2 Cor. 5:21). He continues, now, among other things, to sustain and strengthen you, thereby guaranteeing that you really will be guiltless (see 1 Cor. 1:4–9).

That's why Paul can write to the Corinthians as confidently as he does. Read through his first letter, and you'll be unimpressed with them. They were a mess: divisive (see 1 Cor. 1–3), immoral (see 1 Cor. 5), uncharitable (see 1 Cor. 6), immature (see 1 Cor. 8), arrogant (see 1 Cor. 6:12; 10:23), and exclusive (see 1 Cor. 11). There would be no hope for them if their future were based on how well they had lived out their faith so far.

But Paul is full of hope. He has the audacity to say that one day they will be guiltless—blameless—as they stand before God. That will be their future because of what God has done by calling them into a relationship with his Son. Their goodness doesn't determine the future strength of God's feelings for them. It's the other way around: God's love for them determines their future. Their faith and how they live it out is important—even necessary—but even more necessary is God's prior faithfulness that makes and keeps them faithful. Their (many) current failings don't define them, because those failings don't dictate what they will be. God does. What marks him is his faithfulness to you, and what marks your relationship with him is his faithfulness to you.

So how can you feel his love when you fail? Turn around. Face the future. Meditate on what it will mean for you to be guiltless—on the fact that one day there will not be one voice, including your own, that will ever accuse you again. Meditate on what Jesus did, and is doing, to turn that future into reality. Keep refocusing yourself on Christ until what he has done right begins to feel at least as real as what you have done wrong. When that happens, you will feel his love more deeply than you have before.

> **Reflect:** Whose actions do you tend to think about more often: yours or Christ's?
>
> **Act:** Make a list of as many specific things as you can that Jesus did and is doing to guarantee your future.
>
> **Act:** What will it mean for you to live today looking to your future instead of at your past?

DAY 28

"I Just Know That God Has to Be Fed Up with Me"

I am sure of this, that he who began a good work in you will bring it to completion at the day of Jesus Christ. (Phil. 1:6)

ONE OF THE major difficulties we have with believing that God loves us is that we think he's a lot like us.

We love starting over. We tell ourselves that what's needed is a fresh start, and so we throw ourselves into new relationships and situations. We trade romantic partners, begin friendships, move into different neighborhoods, and give ourselves to new jobs with starry-eyed enthusiasm, certain that these relationships and settings will be better than what we've left behind.

Then reality settles in. Our new friends let us down. The neighborhood doesn't feel as warm and welcoming as it once did. The new company has its own dysfunctional ways of doing things that pinch us in different ways. Everyone knows exactly what we mean when we sigh, "Yeah, the honeymoon is over."

But then we start looking around all over again, wondering, "Is the grass over there less brown than it is here?"

We all do this. So it's not surprising that we expect God to feel the same way toward us—"Surely at some point he has to realize the mistake he made getting involved with me and will decide he is ready to move on." We mistake him for a Pollyannaish optimist who is hopelessly naïve and hasn't yet had a strong enough dose of reality to turn him into a jaded cynic . . . like the rest of us. We look at the hard-heartedness and half-heartedness that we offer him and cannot imagine him—or anyone—hanging in with us, much less passionately loving us.

We get trapped because we make too much of ourselves and too little of him. We see the mess and failure of our lives as being too great for anything to reshape them. And we see the strength of his commitment to us as being too weak to match the self-destructiveness that we carry inside.

It's time to give him more credit.

God is not surprised that your life doesn't perfectly reflect his glory. But he does intend it to. Jesus did not die for the mere possibility that you might end up a little bit better than you used to be. He died to guarantee that one day you would be pure and perfect, just like him.

One thing stands out throughout Scripture: everything that God starts, he finishes. When he brought you into a relationship with himself, he first committed himself to finishing the work that he would begin in you (see Phil. 1:6). His commitment to you not only predates your commitment to him; it is the foundation upon which your commitment is built (see Eph. 1:4, 11–12).

Be confident then. One day you will love him just as fully and completely as he loves you.

Reflect: In your friendship with Christ, do you spend more time thinking about your relational weaknesses and failures or about his relational strengths?

Reflect: Jesus is much more committed to you than you are to the sin that keeps you from him.

Act: Make a list, from Scripture and from your personal life, of all the ways that Jesus has shown how committed he is to you.

DAY 29

"But What If I've Denied Knowing Christ?"

And the Lord turned and looked at Peter. And Peter
remembered the saying of the Lord, how he had said to him,
"Before the rooster crows today, you will deny me three times."
And he went out and wept bitterly. (Luke 22:61–62)

PERHAPS YOU ARE thinking, "Some of this book is helpful, but you don't understand. I'm not struggling with uncertain thoughts or feelings. What I've done is much worse. I rejected Christ."

Maybe people were openly mocking faith and then asked you if you believed in God, and you just shook your head. Or maybe you gave your life to Christ until something else caught your attention—a guy, a girl, a substance, a lifestyle, a passion, a career—and you turned your back on everything that had to do with God. You stopped talking with him, drinking in Scripture, being with his people, and caring about his kingdom, because you found life in this other thing. You may not have said the words, but your actions screamed, "I never knew him."

Now, however, you want him. You hate that you disowned him—but there's no denying that you did. You wish you could turn back the clock and make different decisions, but you can't.

You are in good company. Not only did the crowds abandon Jesus, but so did every one of his disciples, including his three closest friends: Peter, James, and John. To his shame, Peter repeatedly and emphatically denied any connection to Jesus—despite claiming earlier that he couldn't possibly fall away, that he would choose imprisonment and death over denial (see Luke 22:33). All the rest of the disciples agreed and said the same thing (see

Matt. 26:35)—and they were no more successful at carrying out their commitment than Peter was.

Far from being surprised, Jesus knew that his followers would do this. He even predicted it (see Matt. 26:31). Even better, he told them that he had already solved the problem they were about to create. Jesus had prayed that their faith would not fail (see Luke 22:31–32). Let that sink in: their denials would not end their faith. They believed before they denied Jesus, and they would continue believing afterward because of what he had done.

But Jesus didn't stop with prayer. He pursued them. After rising from the dead, he sent them a message—singling Peter out by name—to let them know where he'd meet up with them (see Mark 16:7). Christ met them, called them his brothers, and restored Peter (see John 21:15–19).

That's encouraging—but how do you know whether he'll do the same for you? Look at Peter. When his denial sinks in, Peter weeps bitterly. That shows you that his denial ran counter to the man of faith God had made him to be. It tells you that his restoration is just around the corner—that Jesus will keep his promise to restore Peter.

Are you saddened at denying Christ? Do you wish that you never had? Do you wish you could turn back the clock and do something different? Then be confident. Jesus has prayed for you and will restore you, too.

Reflect: Do you have greater faith in the strength of your commitment to Christ or in the strength of his commitment to you?

Reflect: Do the times that you have denied Christ, either explicitly or through your lifestyle, upset you?

Act: Thank Jesus for the gift of sadness over your unfaithfulness. Tell him how thrilled you are that he's working to restore your faith.

DAY 30

Are You Growing in the Fruit of the Spirit?

For if these qualities [virtue, knowledge, self-control, steadfastness, godliness, brotherly affection, and love] are yours and are increasing, they keep you from being ineffective or unfruitful in the knowledge of our Lord Jesus Christ. (2 Peter 1:8)

PLANTS GROW. THE only time they stop doing so is when they start to die. Animals also grow. They not only increase in size but also mature internally as they gain greater life experience. All they need is food and a decent environment, and they grow. And human beings grow. It's what we do. No one needs to command us to grow. If we have what we need to sustain life, then we develop physically, mentally, and emotionally, learning to master ourselves and the larger world. It's part of the nature of being alive.

That doesn't mean that growth is always at the same speed or in the same area. Nor are you necessarily aware that you're growing. In fact, it's often easier to see growth by comparing the past with the present than by trying to assess it in the moment. But growth happens. It happens because it's built into living. To live is to grow. You can't help it.

That's true of your spirit as well. When God's Spirit lives in you, he causes your spirit to grow (see 2 Peter 1:8). Once God has birthed your spirit, you develop and mature spiritually (see 2 Cor. 3:18). You see that in two ways.

First, you see aspects of God's character—the fruit of his Spirit—in your life where you didn't see them before (see Gal. 5:16–24). You are patient or kind or sacrificial or courageous in ways that surprise you. You don't complain about a hardship that previously would have upset you. You respond to life in ways that look an awful lot like the ways God responds.

Second, you see those budding traits of the Spirit getting larger (see 2 Thess. 1:3). Your patience expands. Your capacity to endure difficulties increases. It's not as hard to give yourself away. You stand up for others and to others more easily. You see more and more of God's character in your life the longer you know him.

Now beware: the enemy of your soul will try to blind you to the importance of growth. He'll distract you by saying, "Hey, did you see what So-and-so just did? They're so much better than you are . . . are you sure you're really a Christian?"

That's when you need to stop thinking about So-and-so and think instead about your own life. Do you see any love, joy, peace, patience, kindness, or self-control in you where there used to be none? Do you see any of them growing stronger? If so, you can confidently respond, "It may be true that I'm not what So-and-so is, but I'm also not what I once was. I'm growing."

Look for growth and development in the fruit of the Spirit in your life rather than trying to measure yourself against someone else's level of godliness. What you see may not be as much or as developed as you'd like, but seeing any goodness at all indicates that God is at work. He's making you grow like a normal, healthy child of his so that you become like your heavenly Father.

Reflect: Do you see any evidence of God's character in you? Then thank him that he's given you his Spirit and that you're growing.

Reflect: Do you see any evidence that you've developed more of his character now than you used to have? Then thank him and ask him to grow you even more.

DAY 31

God Is in It for the Long Haul

Then [God] said, "Let me go, for the day has broken." But Jacob said, "I will not let you go unless you bless me." (Gen. 32:26)

NONE OF US has a brilliant track record when it comes to pursuing God wholeheartedly and consistently. All of us have had our own seasons of being indifferent or even antagonistic toward him.

But what if you've had an overabundance of those times? What if God decides that you're too much of a handful, too high maintenance, too needy, too stubborn, or too difficult to work with? What if he thinks he's had too little return on his investment and says, "You know what? I gave it a good try, but we're done here"?

Abraham's grandson, Jacob, did his best to wear God out. God chose him, before he was born, to be the next link in the chain that would eventually bring Christ to earth (see Gen. 25:23). But Jacob didn't show much promise as a man of faith. He cheated his older brother out of his birthright, then stole the family blessing from him by deceiving their father. While he knew about God, he demonstrated no personal relationship with him (see Gen. 27:20) or confidence that God would protect his life. So he skipped town.

If you do the math, Jacob was seventy-seven years old at the time. That's a long time to live in the tents of God's people and have no faith to show for it. But that didn't deter God. He appeared to Jacob as he was running away and reaffirmed his intention to bless all the nations through him, promising to be with him, to guard him, and to bring him back safely (see Gen. 28:13–15).

Jacob left for twenty years. Those twenty years show ugly things about this man, but they reveal something else as well.

They show small stirrings of faith that prove that God has been with him and has been keeping his promise. After those two decades, God tells Jacob to return home and physically grapples with him one dark night on the way. It is then, after he's nearly a century old, that you finally hear Jacob desire God more than he desires anything else.

God told him, "Let me go," but Jacob said, "Not until you bless me." After a lifetime of trying to fill his hands with the things of this world, Jacob has decided that what he really wants to hold on to—what he really wants more than anything else—is God himself.

When did he get saved? Who knows? What we do know is that God hung in with him until he was a completely different person.

What is most crucial to persevering in your faith is God persevering with you. God pursues you and wrestles with you to guarantee the payoff that he desires—for you to want him just as much as he wants you. Yes, most likely you have wandered from him—probably multiple times. But ask yourself, "Do I still want him?" The answer is obvious: of course you do. That's why you picked up this book and read it through. Those are glimmers of faith that tell you that he has not given up on you. They tell you that he is still invested in you.

Grab on to him in return, and set your mind at rest: the Lord commits himself to his people for the long haul so that they commit to him.

Reflect: Has something else captured your heart other than Christ? Are you following him half-heartedly?

Act: If God can transform Jacob, he can transform you too. Ask the Lord for the grace to hold on to him as tightly as he holds on to you.

Conclusion

Your New Life Is Far More Powerful than Your Doubts

As a Christian, you live an in-between life. Right now you are part of the New Creation (see 2 Cor. 5:17). You have been united with Christ, and you take part in his divine nature (see 2 Peter 1:3–4). But you are not yet fully mature (see Eph. 4:11–13), and you still wrestle with an active sin nature amid a world of temptation (see Gal. 5:16–17).

Both realities, though seemingly contradictory, are true—but they are not equally strong. The life that God has birthed into you is far more powerful than the world of evil and darkness, though sometimes it doesn't seem like it—especially when you've been overwhelmed by temptation or given in to sin.

Thankfully, God isn't as blinded or distracted by our perceptions of reality as we are. The Lord continues gently, steadily moving us toward the goal he has always had of fitting us perfectly into the coming age.

Nothing you have done—not one thing—has thrown him a curve or caused him to rethink his plans. God is not frustrated with you. He is not fretting. He is not upset or furious. He knew exactly what he was getting into when he tied himself to you, and he knew that he would be enough to transform you into the gloriously faithful person that you want to be.

But he accomplishes that future for you without running roughshod over you. He doesn't compel you into holiness against your will, which means that there are times when you do things that aren't always in line with the person you are becoming. Those experiences open the door to doubt—to wondering whether or not you really are saved.

How do you handle your failings to keep in step with Christ? They should move you to sorrow, but not to despair. Coming short of the perfections of Christ is a tragedy, and each failing should be mourned as such. But after Christ's resurrection, each one of his people's lives end joyfully. God's children triumphantly overcome all obstacles, regardless of how many tragic elements we or others choose to write into the story.

Give God the Credit He Deserves

If you forget the controlling narrative—and, most importantly, who controls the narrative—you will arrogate too much responsibility to yourself. And that's easy to do without being aware of it. A woman whom I was counseling found it really helpful when I told her, "You have much greater confidence in your ability to ruin your life than in God's ability to rescue you from yourself and to redeem you."

Can you relate to her? I can. Far too often I think too highly of my own abilities to pursue Christ, to desire holiness, to be faithful, and to live righteously. The flip side of that equation is that I think far too little of God's Spirit and the work he is doing in me. I give myself too much credit while giving him far too little.

The solution is not to care less about holiness or sanctification—not to say, "Okay, Jesus has saved me—therefore it doesn't matter how I live." The solution is to learn to see that, as active as you are in your life, God is much more so. It's to remember that you didn't earn a place in God's family—but that you do have one. You have one because that's what God wanted for you.

Look, then, for evidence of his desire in Scripture, and meditate on it—turning it over and over in your mind until it sinks more deeply into your soul. Look to see that your Messiah, your Savior, has done whatever is necessary to free you from the power of sin. Look to see the resources he has given you to turn his eternal goal of being with you into a daily, livable reality. Then, in light of all he has done and provided, look at the things that you're afraid will get in the way of what he wants for you—and see them for the weak and flimsy things that they truly are.

What Should You Remember?

Realize that nothing now stands between you and God, and that nothing ever can. Jesus did everything he did for you because the Father wanted you so badly. Together they send their Spirit into your heart to remind you of what's true and to empower you to live in line with that truth. Focus on those things and you will feel God's love—and can know that it will never be taken from you.

And make sure that you look at his attitude as he does all these things for you. Remember what was prophesied about Christ: that "a bruised reed he will not break, and a faintly burning wick he will not quench" (Isa. 42:3). Remember how he lived out that prophecy both with his close friends and also with complete strangers. Remember that he is the same person today that he was yesterday and will be forever.

Remember that his gentleness with people's faith struggles so marked him that it makes sense for Jude to urge God's people to "have mercy on those who doubt" (Jude 22). Mercy to the doubting must characterize God's people, because it characterizes God.

That admonition does not simply apply to how you should treat others who doubt. Embrace it as the way to treat yourself— then run to the one whose demeanor invited a man to cry to him, "I believe; help my unbelief!" (Mark 9:24). Jesus healed that man's son, demonstrating that he also did the harder thing—he healed the man's unbelief.

This is the God you are dealing with—one who knows how to love real people who can't clean themselves up. Focus on his love, and remember that perfect love casts out all fear (see 1 John 4:18). Focusing on the fear, or on things that generate fear, will keep you spiritually paralyzed and demoralized. Focus instead on the love—on a God who knows you will struggle with many doubts and who has committed himself to loving you out of every last one of them.

Suggested Resources
for the Journey

John Bunyan, *The Pilgrim's Progress.*

In this allegory, Bunyan portrays his main character, Christian, journeying through places that feel very familiar to anyone who has tried to live the life of faith: the Slough of Despond, the Valley of Humiliation, the Valley of the Shadow of Death, and Doubting Castle—where Giant Despair not only imprisons Christian but torments him as well.

Along the way, Christian meets many familiar types of people—Pliable, Mr. Worldly Wiseman, Timorous, and Ignorance, to name a few—who each suggest that there's an easier road to the Celestial City than the one he is on. At times, Christian listens to their bad advice. At other times, he gives in to his own temptations or is worn down by wrestling with the devil. These, again, are all common experiences for the person who is following Christ.

But he also encounters unlooked-for friends who encourage him in his journey—Evangelist, Interpreter, Faithful, and Hopeful—and receives help that is sent by the Lord just when he needs it most.

Bunyan's pictures and descriptions help you to realize that the intense struggles and doubts you have are normal for God's people. That is comforting. Even more helpful is the realization that the worst never lasts, because the true King provides everything that his pilgrims need to be with him forever.

Os Guinness, *God in the Dark: The Assurance of Faith Beyond a Shadow of Doubt* (Wheaton, IL: Crossway, 1996).

Guinness decouples doubt from unbelief, arguing that doubting is normal when faith and unbelief both seem to provide equally valid answers to life's difficulties. He explains that you resolve this quandary by understanding God as he truly is. When you see the real God, not only do you see the inadequacy of unbelief but you move toward him relationally because you want more of him personally.

Guinness compassionately addresses several categories of doubts—first tackling those that arise at the outset of faith and then proceeding to ones that crop up along the journey of faith. His systematic treatment builds a foundation for believing that God is, and remains, faithful to his people.

Donald S. Whitney, *How Can I Be Sure I'm a Christian? What the Bible Says About Assurance of Salvation* (Colorado Springs: NavPress, 1994).

Whitney argues that the assurance of salvation sits firmly on the foundation of what God has done to rescue his people from their sins as revealed in Scripture. Any other attempt to secure or be confident of God's love—such as relying on your own moral efforts or pursuing spiritual experiences—must leave you uncertain of his attitude toward you.

Whitney's short but comprehensive treatment of assurance is essentially a readable theology of salvation—what it is, how to obtain it, evidences of it, and how to discern when it's genuine or counterfeit, along with practical suggestions about what to do if you continue to deal with lingering doubts that God, in his mercy, has rescued you.

BIBLICAL
COUNSELING
COALITION

The Biblical Counseling Coalition (BCC) is passionate about enhancing and advancing biblical counseling globally. We accomplish this through broadcasting, connecting, and collaborating.

Broadcasting promotes gospel-centered biblical counseling ministries and resources to bring hope and healing to hurting people around the world. We promote biblical counseling in a number of ways: through our *15:14* podcast, website (biblicalcounselingcoalition.org), partner ministry, conference attendance, and personal relationships.

Connecting biblical counselors and biblical counseling ministries is a central component of the BCC. The BCC was founded by leaders in the biblical counseling movement who saw the need for and the power behind building a strong global network of biblical counselors. We introduce individuals and ministries to one another to establish gospel-centered relationships.

Collaboration is the natural outgrowth of our connecting efforts. We truly believe that biblical counselors and ministries can accomplish more by working together. The BCC Confessional Statement, which is a clear and comprehensive definition of biblical counseling, was created through the cooperative effort of over thirty leading biblical counselors. The BCC has also published a three-part series of multi-contributor works that bring theological wisdom and practical expertise to pastors, church leaders, counseling practitioners, and students. Each year we are able to facilitate the production of numerous resources, including books, articles, videos, audio resources, and a host of other helps for biblical counselors. Working together allows us to provide robust resources and develop best practices in biblical counseling so that we can hone the ministry of soul care in the church.

To learn more about the BCC, visit biblicalcounselingcoalition.org.

More from P&R Publishing

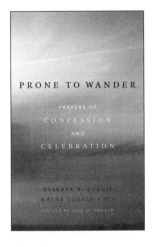
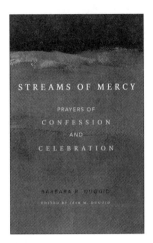

Confessing our sins might seem like a gloomy business . . . but exposing the specifics of our struggles with sin leads to celebration! It points us back to the good news of the gospel, our great Savior, and our forgiveness through God's grace.

Inspired by the Puritan classic *The Valley of Vision*, the prayers in these two volumes are ideal for use in church services or personal devotions. They open with a scriptural call of confession, confess specific sins, thank the Father for Jesus' perfect life and death in our place, ask for the help of the Spirit in pursuing holiness, and close with an assurance of pardon.

"[*Prone to Wander*] has many virtues. . . . The book covers the whole of the Christian life. I love its overall aims and method."
—Leland Ryken

"Here we learn how to pray God's Word back to him . . . and celebrate his grace in so many areas of our lives. I recommend [*Streams of Mercy*] strongly."
—John Frame

Was this book helpful to you?
Consider writing a review online.
The author appreciates your feedback!

Or write to P&R at editorial@prpbooks.com
with your comments. We'd love to hear from you.